THE LIBRARY OF POLITICAL ECONOMY

POLITICAL ECONOMY is the old name for economics. In the hands of the great classical economists, particularly Smith, Ricardo and Marx, economics was the study of the working and development of the economic system in which men and women lived. Its practitioners were driven by a desire to describe, to explain and to evaluate what they saw around them. No sharp distinction was drawn between economic analysis and economic policy nor between economic behaviour and its interaction with the technical, social and political framework.

The Library of Political Economy has been established to provide widely based explanations of economic behaviour in contemporary society.

In examining the way in which new patterns of social organization and behaviour influence the economic system and policies for combating problems associated with growth, inflation, poverty and the distribution of wealth, contributors stress the link between politics and economics and the importance of institutions in policy formulation.

This 'open-ended' approach to economics implies that there are few laws that can be held to with certainty and, by the same token, there is no generally established body of theory to be applied in all circumstances. Instead economics as presented in this library provides a way of ordering events which has constantly to be updated and modified as new situations develop. This, we believe, is its interest and its challenge.

Urban Inequalities under State Socialism

Ivan Szelenyi

WITHDRAWN

OXFORD UNIVERSITY PRESS
1983

Oxford University Press, Walton Street, Oxford OX2 6DP
London Glasgow New York Toronto
Delhi Bombay Calcutta Madras Karachi
Kuala Lumpur Singapore Hong Kong Tokyo
Nairobi Dar es Salaam Cape Town
Melbourne Auckland
and associated companies in
Beirut Berlin Ibadan Mexico City Nicosia

Oxford is a trade mark of Oxford University Press

Published in the United States by
Oxford University Press, New York

British Library Cataloguing in Publication Data
Szelenyi, Ivan
 Urban inequalities under state socialism.
 —(The Library of political economy)
 1. Sociology, Urban
 I. Title II. Series
 307.7'6'0947   HT153
 ISBN 0-19-877175-4
 ISBN 0-19-877176-2 Pbk

Library of Congress Cataloging in Publication Data
Szelényi, Iván.
 Urban inequalities under state
socialism.
 (The Library of political economy)
 Originally published as the author's Ph.D.
thesis.
 Bibliography: p.
 Includes index.
 1. Sociology, Urban—Case studies.
 2. Equality—Case studies. 3. Socialism—Europe,
Eastern. 4. Cities and towns—Europe, Eastern.
 5. Szeged (Hungary)—Social conditions. 6. Pécs
(Hungary)—Social conditions. I. Title II. Series.
 HT151.S95 1983   307.7'6   82-12515
 ISBN 0-19-877175-4
 ISBN 0-19-877176-2 (pbk.)

Typeset by Oxprint Ltd, Oxford
Printed in Hong Kong

Preface

THIS book is based mainly on data from a survey I carried out with George Konrad in Hungary, in Pecs and Szeged in 1968. Then, during 1969–72, I collected as many comparative data as I could from other countries of Eastern Europe, and included all those I found useful in this book. The data thus represent only two cities systematically, and some others patchily; and they are already some years old. The work was originally finished in May 1972. It earned me a Ph.D. degree, but I was already beginning to have political difficulties and no Hungarian publishing house would risk publishing it.

I left Hungary in 1975. Some of my ideas have changed since then, and so no doubt have some of the urban facts. I might have tried to re-write the book—but it would have been a different book. Though I might write somewhat differently today, I take responsibility for the book as it is.

In preparing to publish it now for the first time I have decided not to change the text to any significant extent. A few outdated references have been omitted; there have been some changes from present to past tense, and some shorter phrasing, in the course of translation. The bibliography lists only the sources available at that time, and of those, only the ones referred to in the text. I hope the human ecologists will forgive the simple-minded statistical techniques I used, but at the time they seemed sufficient for this sort of policy-oriented research.

As a kind of compromise I have written a new introduction to replace the original and longer theoretical introduction. I hope this may help Western readers to identify the political and ideological assumptions and values which underlie the empirical and analytical chapters. But, from Chapter 1 to Chapter 7 the book stands substantially as it was written: a critical assessment of East European socialist institutions, written by an East European employed at the time by an East European government.

Adelaide,
August 1979   IVAN SZELENYI

Acknowledgements

Most of the ideas for this book were developed with George Konrad with whom I conducted the empirical research upon which the analysis is based. I would also like to express my thanks to Hugh Stretton who encouraged me to publish this manuscript in English, offered valuable editorial advice, and spent a great deal of time in improving the English translation. Finally, my thanks are due to my daughter Szonja Szelenyi who helped with the translation and compiled the index.

I. Szelenyi

Contents

Part II.   Urban Planning and Social Structure

List of Figures

Introduction: Notes on the Nature of Cities in Socialist Eastern Europe

Comments on the concept of 'socialist cities'

This book is about cities under existing socialism, about socialist cities. The purpose of the research upon which the book is based—a sociological survey of two middle-sized Hungarian cities, Pecs and Szeged—was to try to understand what socialism did to cities, to their inhabitants, and especially to the urban poor in Eastern Europe. This book is an empirical account and not an ideological statement. I will not attempt to present a vision of the 'good city', which is what most of my colleagues usually do when they speak about 'socialist cities'. Using the two Hungarian cities as case studies, I will try to show in what respects cities in socialist Eastern Europe are different from cities elsewhere, and different from what they themselves used to be.

I call these cities 'socialist' on empirical grounds. They are socialist in the following senses. Firstly, the cities in socialist Eastern Europe are different from the places they used to be before the Second World War. Secondly, since the socialist transformation of these societies—with nationalization of most means of production, nationalization or at least strict state control of urban land, abolition of the 'commodity' status of urban housing and other means of collective consumption—the urban changes have been quite different from those of neighbouring non-socialist countries. For example, Budapest and Vienna, not all that different at the turn of the century or at the eve of the Second World War, are changing in different directions now. Thirdly, cities in socialist Eastern Europe are becoming more alike, even if their historical traditions made them differ in the past. Go for a walk in a new housing development in Budapest, Prague, and Moscow—it will take you some time to find out which country you are in. Visit a fellow sociologist in East Berlin or Warsaw—the size of his flat will be about the same as yours in Budapest or Sofia, he will pay about the same proportion of his income as you do for rent, you could probably swap furniture without noticing a change. Try to buy a pair of shoes, catch a taxi, or order a lunch in a restaurant— you can expect similar experiences in all the cities of Eastern Europe, including cities whose ways of life and business were quite different thirty, fifty, or a hundred years ago. Pecs, Szeged, Warsaw, Bratislava, or other cities in Eastern Europe are 'socialist' not in the sense that they are necessarily better or worse than they used to be, or better or worse than comparable cities in capitalist countries. They are socialist in that they are *different*.

The main purpose of this book is to explore *how different* urban development is under East European socialism. And, since it is a sociological analysis—or what some in the West might prefer to call an exercise in political economy—the main question it asks, over and over, is: 'Who benefits from the differences . . . and who has to pay for them?' The research which led to the book was prompted by some previous investigations which seemed to suggest that the cities of contemporary Eastern Europe are not unequal in the way that other cities are else-where in the world. The purpose of the survey of Pecs and Szeged was to try to find out if indeed a *new pattern of urban inequalities* can be detected and related to socialist economic and social policies. Although the survey was made in 1968, and most of the manuscript was written in 1972, I believe these questions and the answers to them are still central to the current theoreti-cal debate within the new urban sociology, between its 'Marxist' and 'Weberian' representatives. I also believe that the empirical substance of our study retains its interest as a case-study of 'real' socialism.

The new urban sociology and the urban problems under socialism and capitalism

The British sociologist Ray Pahl (Pahl, 1977) keeps reminding his Marxist colleagues that they ought to develop a theory of urbanization under socialism if they want to go on explaining the West's urban problems as products of the capitalist mode of production. In a number of convincing essays Pahl has shown that the differences between urban patterns in the West and in Eastern Europe cannot be fully or sufficiently explained merely by comparing a 'capitalist mode of production' with a 'socialist mode of production'. Manuel Castells himself seems to be aware of the problem. Already in *The Urban Question* (first published in 1972) he observed:

On this basis, designating a society as capitalist, then specifying the precise conjunction and the stage of capitalism that is revealed in it, enables me to organize my analysis theoretically. But the reverse is not true: to designate a social formation as 'socialist' does not elucidate its relation to space and, very often, it tends to divert research, which takes refuge in a series of ideological dichotomies tending to present the obverse side of the capitalist logic, instead of showing the real processes that are developing in the new social forms. The reason for this difference in the analytical capacity of the two categories appears fairly clear: whereas the theory of the capitalist mode of production has been elaborated . . . the theory of the socialist mode of production exists only in an embryonic state (p. 64).

But Pahl is not satisfied with such an explanation (Pahl, 1977). As long as Marxists are not able to determine what creates inequalities under socialism, we should not be obliged to accept their belief that all the inequalities in the West are products of 'capitalism'. Pahl's particular kind of critique leads him to emphasize the similarities between East and West, between capitalism and socialism. He quotes research evidence from Eastern Europe (including some of my own publications) to suggest that, because cities of East and West have similar inequalities, and some similar problems, the problems and inequalities must presumably be created by common forces— forces which operate under both capitalism and socialism. His most radical suggestion is that it is not the mode of production which explains urban processes, but rather the level of production. Technology after all is not innocent, and technology may be more directly responsible for the urban problems than 'relations of production'.

I agree with Pahl's methodological philosophy. I cannot claim that the 'urban problems' of the West issue from the contradictions of the capitalist mode of production, and maintain at the same time that 'urban problems' under socialism do not express structural contradictions but only 'historical conjunctures'. Castells, for example, goes as far as to call the Soviet housing crisis 'conjunctural', and to argue that 'as the economy improved' a whole series of measures were put into effect to solve the conjunctural problem (1977, p. 66). Pahl's objections hold: if I analyse capitalist housing systems as devices for the reproduction of labour power and thus of the whole economic system, then I ought to apply the same logic to socialist housing systems. Castells does acknowledge that the housing crisis afflicted the Soviet Union for at least four decades (is it over yet?); so it becomes reasonable to assume that it is *created by* the Soviet economic system, as a product of its structural contradictions.

Cities under socialism are also unequal

I also agree with Pahl that there are some similar urban contradictions in the West and in Eastern Europe and that some of them are created by technological factors which are comparatively neutral to the modes of production. On the other hand, I think these similarities are banal, while the differences are more interesting and important. For purposes of sociological analysis, for example, we do not get far by establishing that cities are unequal both in the West and in Eastern Europe. That no longer surprises anyone, not even 'fundamentalist communists' —most Soviet ideologues accept that there are 'still' inequalities in their societies. Nor—I confess—do I find much fascination in comparisons of the degrees of inequality. What is really interesting is the *quality* of the new inequalities. That is why this book tries to establish the new patterns of urban social inequalities. I have tried especially to identify those inequalities which (1) were not inherited from 'the capitalist past', and (2) were not maintained by surviving market mechanisms, or other persisting or re-emerging forces of capitalism. Instead of capitalist legacies I have looked for inequalities which are new, which are emerging rather than withering away, which are not alien from the essence of the socialist economy, but which arise logically from the socialist system of production and distribution. When the following chapters of this book were written there had been no opportunity to read *The Urban Question*, yet I find that I did what Castells thought we ought to do—I attempted to 'show the real processes that are developing in the new social forms'.

It is not obvious, to begin with, that such inequalities should actually exist. The idea of socialism is associated with the idea of equality and it seems to be an irreconcilable contradiction to suggest that genuine socialist measures can unavoidably generate inequalities. It took me some time before I began formulating this hypothesis for my research. It may be of interest to give a short account of that experience, for scientific reasons. More generally, English-speaking readers may like to know something of the everyday conditions of intellectual life in Eastern Europe. So I offer the following summary of the experience which led to the research on which this book is based.

I conducted the first major empirical urban research in 1966–7. In late 1965 or early 1966 I met George Konrad, who at that time had just taken up a position as an urban sociologist in an urban and regional planning institute. I had a job as a sociologist at the Hungarian Academy of Sciences and was expected to become a specialist in urban sociology. We were both inexperienced, but I had some knowledge of the literature and of survey methodology and Konrad had sufficient funds through his institution. We decided to join forces and conduct joint researches. We did not have a very clear idea of what we ought to do, so we did not mind when our urban planning colleagues suggested that we investigate new housing estates. In 1966 and 1967 we organized a number of fairly large-scale surveys on four new housing developments in Budapest and in three provincial towns. We did not really have a proper research design: our studies were basically descriptive; we did not know what kind of questions we should ask. In the end we put together a lengthy questionnaire which contained all sorts of foolish questions, but at least we did not forget to ask our respondents to state their occupation, incomes, etc. So we got some decent data about their stratificational position, and that did enable us to establish who lived in the new housing estates, if only in a purely descriptive way. But the simple facts themselves were interesting enough. In Hungarian cities, as in all cities in Eastern Europe, most new housing is financed and built by the state, and is then administratively allocated at a highly subsidized rent to those who 'need' new housing. This new state housing is almost exclusively concentrated on new high-density housing estates. Therefore, by studying new housing developments you see in concentrated form the most distinctive urban effects of the socialist transformation.

When we had collected our data, we began our analysis of it

by asking for a great number of cross-tabulations of the items relating to the population composition of the estates. I still remember the first day when Konrad and I sat down in his flat and started to look at the computer print-outs. We just could not believe our eyes. I was quite sure that something had gone wrong with the computer—this was the first time we had used a computer and it had taken a couple of months to get any print-out from it at all. And here it was trying to tell us that it is mainly the middle class—clerical workers, professionals, intellectuals, bureaucrats, and the like—who live on these housing developments. Skilled workers are reasonably well represented, but the bulk of the working class is nowhere to be seen. This meant that the state housing was being allocated to the higher income groups and not to the proletariat. Neither Konrad nor I were ever 'believers' and we had never thought much of East European communism—but, even for us, this was too much from 'the dictatorship of the proletariat'. To some extent at least, we had accepted the official line that state housing is allocated according to need, and we therefore expected to find a fairly-balanced population in the new housing. But there was no computer error and a number of investigations proved that new state housing is indeed allocated systematically to the higher income groups. That suggested two conclusions: *housing inequalities are being created now*, as those with higher incomes get the better housing; and *these inequalities are being created by administrative allocation*, i.e. by the distinctively socialist mechanism which was supposed to replace the capitalist market method of allocation.

This was perhaps not a big discovery, but it was a discovery: somehow these facts were just not known. Curiously enough, even the housing authorities who allocated the housing did not keep reliable statistics of those who received it, and from population censuses and existing sociological surveys it was not possible to know exactly what kinds of housing were occupied by the different strata of society. I do not really think this was the result of any conspiracy—no one ever attempted to prevent us from collecting our new data, and the first publications of our survey results were well received. Indeed, in 1969 the most prestigious scientific publisher in Hungary, the publishing house of the Hungarian Academy of Sciences, published our book, *Sociological Problems of New Housing Developments* (Szelenyi

and Konrad, 1969). I simply believe that those concerned—
even including the bureaucrats themselves who allocated the
new housing—honestly believed that they gave most of the
housing to the working class, and felt no particular need to
gather systematic data.

I have to add that the situation was quite similar in other
East European countries—unequal allocation of housing
through the state, lack of systematic data, and ignorant experts.
After I had collected enough data in Hungary I decided to visit
other East European countries to see how housing allocation
worked with them. With a grant for the purpose from the
Hungarian Academy of Sciences I visited all East European
socialist countries, except Albania, but including the Soviet
Union. First of all the data just did not exist, even in countries
where urban sociology was highly developed; even in Czechoslovakia and Poland I found only unsystematic and often
indirect evidence. (Needless to say I got no data at all from
countries like the USSR or Bulgaria.) But what I found even
more interesting was the misconception some leading experts
had concerning the social consequences of housing allocation. I
had a long discussion with a leading Polish urban sociologist,
a fine gentleman who seemed more like a Polish nobleman than
a 'devoted communist'. He was genuinely surprised to hear
about our findings in Hungary. 'How interesting', he thought,
'to see what differences there are among socialist countries.
Here in Poland what you just described would be unimagin-
able.' And he explained to me at some length that in Poland
only the workers had access to new housing. True, he himself
happened to live in a new flat, but his neighbour was a driver—
in a ministry. Experiences of that sort are doubly depressing.
First of all it is disappointing that, in a country like Poland, with
a long tradition of sociological research, one has to rely on such
anecdotal evidence when discussing a major social problem
with a leading sociologist. Secondly my Professor X was quite
wrong in his impression of the situation. I did later find data on
three Polish cities. They are included in this book, and they
show emerging patterns of inequality like those we found in
Hungary. Did Professor X lie? I do not think so—two years
earlier I myself would have responded in much the same way to
the same questions.

With our survey of new housing estates we thought we had

discovered new kinds of inequalities which were generated by unexpected mechanisms. We had also come to realize that ultimately it is not the degree of inequality that matters, but the nature of the inequalities. Let me again exemplify this with an anecdote. Late in the 1960s Konrad and I published a paper on housing allocation (Konrad and Szelenyi, 1969). It was generally well received, but one reader began to show concern about our 'funny' kind of investigations, and he happened to be one of the highest ranking officials in the Statistical Office. I met him in the street shortly after the paper was published and he was not very pleased. He asked me: 'Are you suggesting in this paper that I, for example, am privileged by this housing economy?' I assured him that this was indeed our intention. He was quite upset. He lived in a good flat, state-allocated, but he did not think he was privileged. 'Compare my flat with the apartment the official in my position in the Austrian Bureau of Census has in Vienna and then you will see how underprivileged I am.' He had a point. His colleague in Vienna had a much better apartment, and he felt that comparison entitled him to regard the Hungarian housing system as a paradise of equality. But he missed my point: what is interesting in this case is not the degree of inequality, but the way it is created. What is really interesting is the *political economy* of housing inequality.

We became aware that we must develop an analysis of *the whole housing system*, an analysis of the allocation of privileges and costs throughout the housing economy. It was not enough to look only at new state housing, we must analyse all types of housing. We must find out if the inequalities which already exist in the society are increased or decreased by housing policy and the actual operation of the housing economy. What is interesting about the socialist housing policy is that my statistician becomes more privileged 'after housing' than 'before housing', while his colleague in Vienna pays a market price for his apartment, so that his housing arrangements reflect his privileges, but probably do not increase them. When my statistician gets a subsidized flat, housing policy makes him better off; if he were an unskilled labourer, housing policy would do less and worse for him. Thus our reasoning led us to the kind of analysis that the next chapters of this book present in great empirical detail. Our survey of Pecs and Szeged was designed to discover and measure patterns of 'housing mobility', showing how people of different social status are housed, what their housing costs them, and what their chances are of changing position in the housing system. The results enabled us to arrive at a very detailed description of the way in which inequalities are generated through the specifically socialist sectors of the housing economy.

Urban social inequalities are created by new mechanisms under socialism

Already at the time of our research in the new housing estates we suspected that the new mechanisms of inequality were probably at work in other fields besides housing. In a general way the replacement of *market allocation* by *administrative allocation* might merely replace one unequalizing force by another. Specifically, what happened in housing might happen more widely in urban structure. We observed that a significant proportion of the well-off migrants to the new housing estates were coming from the 'zone of transition', an area dating from the turn of the century which surrounds the city centre and is gradually deteriorating both physically and socially. This was almost the classical Western process of slum creation, but with one very significant difference—the 'transitional zone' was not deteriorating because of land speculation; on the contrary, it was impossible to mobilize funds for its redevelopment because the value of central land was *not* acknowledged. The issue is discussed later; I mention it here to indicate how we became convinced that administrative allocation can sometimes *reproduce* the unequalizing market mechanism which it is supposed to replace and reverse.

It is very important to grasp that the inequalities which are produced by the socialist mechanisms of the urban economy cannot be defined as consequences of 'bureaucratic mismanagement', or 'corruption'. In the following chapter on housing I argue at length that, in the conditions of the time and place, housing could scarcely be allocated otherwise. If the costs of housing are not passed through personal incomes, then even the highest income groups will not willingly pay market prices, or real costs, for housing. Instead they rely on what they get as 'presents', 'subsidy', 'fringe-benefits' from the state. The bureaucrat in the state housing authority cannot be expected to withhold new housing from those with high incomes, if their incomes are still insufficient to pay for new housing in the market—if there were a market.

Yugoslavia is—or at least was at the time when we conducted this research—an interesting mixture. In Yugoslavia the wage structures are somewhat different, standing somewhere between a Western market wage system and the wage system of Eastern Europe. The Yugoslavs attempted to experiment with 'market' housing for their rich. But their 'rich' still could not afford to pay 'real' rents, although, because they were expected to pay more, they naturally expected higher standards. The result was interesting: luxury housing was built for the 'rich'; its rents were higher than other rents; but, because incomes were still not sufficiently high, the state still had to subsidize luxury housing more than standard housing.

The basic point is this: inequalities in administrative allocation, and inequalities arising from it, probably became inevitable when the wage policy was set. If wages are set officially to exclude the cost of housing and other public goods and services, then housing and the other goods and services must obviously be allocated to all comers, including those with high incomes. If any of the services happens to be scarce—as new housing must always be, since only a small fraction of the housing stock can be new each year—those scarce goods are always likely to be allocated to the most meritorious citizens in the most essential jobs, who tend to be those with the highest incomes. It could scarcely be otherwise. How could the state say to its rising managers and bureaucrats, 'If you get promoted you will *reduce* your housing chances'?

Let me illustrate this with another concrete example. (I hope these bits of gossip may be forgiven—they are sometimes the clearest way to illustrate the message.) After the invasion of Czechoslovakia the Hungarian Academy of Sciences, encouraged by the party, decided that the ideological discipline of sociology needed strengthening, so they appointed a new Deputy Director to our Institute. They chose a gentleman who had been teaching dialectical materialism in a small technical college in a provincial town; if not a remarkable sociologist, he had undoubted claims as a disciplinarian. He was delighted to accept the job, which was a long and unexpected stride ahead for his career, but he no sooner took it than his difficulties began. He had to move from the provincial town to Budapest. He needed an apartment there, and was soon promised one. But he had other problems. He wanted his widowed mother to live near, but not too near, since his wife and her mother-in-law ... etc. We can pass over the details. He got the two flats he wanted. I calculated that they were together worth some twenty years' income of an average industrial worker. For a while I was upset, and wondered whether to make a fuss about it—but the more I thought about it the more convinced I became that even this rather extreme case should not be regarded as 'corrupt' or 'bureaucratic mismanagement'. Once it is accepted (even with some lingering doubts on my part) that he had to move to Budapest because Hungarian sociology could not survive without him, then all the rest followed necessarily enough.

When, about 1970, still as an East European sociologist, I first met David Donnison and tried to explain to him how the housing system in Eastern Europe operated, he summed up our long discussion in the following way: 'Are you suggesting that we need a market for the rich if we want to help the poor?' That is a very bourgeois way to put it, but quite correct. I myself formulated the problem somewhat differently: while under capitalism the market creates the basic inequalities and the administrative allocation of welfare modifies and moderates them slightly, under socialism the major inequalities are created by administrative allocation, and the market can be used to reduce inequalities. Although I know Charles Bettelheim would not like this argument at all (most Western Marxists will label me another market revisionist, like Bauman or Brus), it is not really very far from what he was trying to tell Paul Sweezy in their celebrated exchange of letters on the problems of transition. It is not planning *per se* or market *per se* that makes socialism socialism: what really matter are the class consequences of economic actions. In a general way I agree, and this book is an attempt to evaluate precisely, and empirically, the class consequences of different measures of urban and housing policy under socialism. It may be revisionist, but it is at least a 'sociology from below'. I would like it to be understood as a socialist critique of existing socialism.

Beyond the problems of distribution—the socialist redistributive regional management system

There is one final point I would like to make in this introduction. The empirical material of this book is mainly on allocation, distribution, access to facilities, etc. But I would be very disappointed if it were treated as relevant only to the problems of distribution or consumption. Castells with his unfortunate concept 'means of collective consumption', (Castells, 1977), has already led too many urban sociologists in the last decade to believe (as I do not think he himself has ever believed) that urban sociology is about consumption and that production has not much to do with cities. That notion is obviously ludicrous and not worth serious consideration. But I am also doubtful about the rigid distinction between 'production' and 'distribution', which has been so implemented among socialists as well as bourgeois theorists, especially since Trotsky. It has been used more recently by David Lane, who suggests that societies may have a socialist form of production, but a bourgeois form of distribution. I disagree; I cannot understand how it might be possible to have 'socialist productive relations' with 'bourgeois distribution'. The processes of distribution or allocation described in this book are unequal, but they are not bourgeois in any meaningful sense of the word, unless bourgeois simply means bad or unequal, and socialist means good or equal. These processes of allocation are socialist. What is more important, they emerge specifically from the socialist method of economic organization: they reflect at the level of distribution the laws of socialist production and reproduction.

Administrative allocation of housing, bureaucratic decisions about how to use urban land, what proportion of the national income should be used for infrastructural development, rather than consumed, the administrative decisions to locate these infrastructural investments in cities or in villages in developed regions or in developing areas, etc.—these are inherent features of the centrally planned socialist economy. In that economy, investment decisions are not designed to maximize profits. Instead they express the central will and its conception of social good. In such systems the movement of labour is not regulated by supply and demand, but by the intentions of the central

hand. When in this book I describe certain patterns of allocation and distribution, I describe the allocative mechanism of
the centrally planned socialist economy, which elsewhere,
following Polanyi's terminology with some modifications
(Polanyi, 1957), I have called the 'redistributive economy' or
the 'economy of rational redistribution'. (In this book the term
'administrative allocation' is commoner, but the difference is
one of translation, and not significant.)

With housing especially, we are not talking only about distribution. The distributive mechanisms are built into the productive systems, and reflect the logic of the productive systems.
When after the investigation in Pecs and Szeged we thought we
could prove beyond doubt that the administrative allocation of
housing is 'disfunctional' in the sense that its results are opposite to its declared aims, we came forward with a policy proposal. We suggested that, all things considered, it is unlikely
that the administrative allocation of housing can be improved,
or transformed into a genuine system of social housing. If more
money is spent on state housing for administrative allocation
(which at the time we called a redistributive housing system) it
will only help the rich. If we want to help the poor we have to
improve the market sector, since the overwhelming majority of
the working class has to house itself on the market anyway. So
we made a most naïve proposal to the Central Planning Office.
We suggested that they should radically cut state housing
construction. They should in future build housing only for the
very poor. But they should relax many of the existing constraints on private housing construction, and the funds they
used up to now for state housing should be offered instead for
mortgage loans. We could prove that this measure would significantly help the working class, and would actually lead to more
housing construction because it would mobilize more of the
personal savings of the population.

It goes without saying that this foolish proposition was never
seriously considered. How can you expect the planners, sitting
in the Central Planning Office or in the Ministry of Housing, to
give up their powers—and their power is measured by the
percentage of the national income they can direct. The administrative allocation of housing means large-scale state housing
construction, it means large construction companies, it means
large planning institutions. It means that decisions about how

much money to spend, where and on what kind of housing, are not taken by the consumers, but by the planners. It means power for the 'teleological planner', power which is not alien to the idea of the centrally planned socialist economy but central to it.

This book is a first step towards a critical analysis of that kind of teleological planning as it manifests itself in the new state socialist system of administrative or redistributive urban management. That system includes central control of the allocation of resources to urban investment and management, and of the detailed use and distribution of those resources. The system is advertised as 'rational management'—and, all too easily, maximizing the central planners' command of the business becomes the only criterion of 'rationality'.

We once hoped to take more than merely the first step. The critical analysis of this new system and its underlying ideologies (and theologies) seemed important enough to attract whatever we could muster of research resources and theoretical inventiveness. But the project was interrupted by forces beyond our control. From Adelaide, South Australia, that particular line of investigation could not be continued. But, although this book and the investigations leading to it are not a mature treatment of the subject, and in particular do not offer a better alternative to the East European system of urban management, I hope they may at least begin to corrode belief in the 'rationality' of 'state socialist rational redistribution'.

A final anecdote: in one of the Urban and Regional Planning Institutes which financed our research, another researcher was also at work on housing. He was a fine old man, at that time specially concerned about the low birth rate and critical of government housing policy. He thought the small new housing units caused the low birth rate, so that the noble Hungarian race might die out, or at least be outnumbered by slaves and gypsies. For a long time he thought we were allies and followed our work with interest. But after discussion of one of our final research reports he came to us and asked: 'Do you recommend that people ought to live wherever they want to live?' We said we thought that really would be terrific. He was deeply shocked. That would lead to anarchy, and be the end of planning. What are we planners doing, what function do we have, if not telling people what they ought to do?

We ourselves began our work with naïve and simple-minded measures of inequalities in new housing, and in the end came close to questioning the very principles upon which the philosophy of planning and the practice of urban management are based in socialist Eastern Europe. We began to question the vanguardist, élitist, 'scientific' type of planning and the economic and social system upon which such planning is based. But we were not and are not anti-planners, and this book is not against planning, and most certainly not against state intervention whose aim is to help the poor, to fight exploitation or prejudice, and reduce inequality. On the contrary, this book is 'sociology from below'. It criticizes the East European performance for using the ideology of equality to create inequality, for making the already-privileged more privileged, and the already-deprived more deprived. This book is not against planning by governments, it is against government by planners. To return to the question of our old patriot friend, it would be good if people could live where and how they want to live. As long as they cannot, it would be great if we could have planners who could help them have more options rather than less. This book is against planning which decides for people and narrows their choices, but it is for planning which extends and adds to their choices. It is for planning whenever it enables people to do more, or to choose from better options than were possible before the planning began.

I have insisted that the inequalities and the underlying system of planning and management analysed in this book are *socialist*. On the other hand I do not accept that this is the only kind of thing that can happen under socialism. I do not accept that there can be no socialist alternative to the East European socio-economic and urban system. This is why the title of this book specifies *state socialism*—a state socialism which represents one kind of post-capitalist society, and one kind of modern industrial society which can function without the institution of private property. I am not convinced that our only choice is between rule by capital or rule by 'teleological redistributors'. I believe that we may yet learn how to govern ourselves. That may well take time, but to proceed at all in that direction we must learn the historic lesson of East European socialism, and we must learn it as a lesson of one form of socialism. I hope this book will make some contribution to that task.

PART I

HOUSING AND SOCIAL STRUCTURE

CHAPTER 1

Housing as a Social Problem

STUDIES, newspaper articles, and books dealing with housing are introduced in words to the effect that 'housing is the most urgent problem of our society'. This proposition appears to be accepted, without need for further proof, by readers everywhere—whether in Hungary, Sweden, the USA, India, the USSR, or Poland. We can deduce from such a consensus that housing is indeed a world problem—but is it really the same problem for Swedes and Americans and Indians? Why should people be equally discontented with their housing, and researchers equally gloomy about housing problems, in countries with completely different housing situations, *per capita* income, and economic development? The Swedes must surely be dissatisfied with a housing situation very different from the housing situation which dissatisfies Hungarians or Indians. An urban Hungarian of average means might be quite pleased with housing judged 'bad' by his Swedish counterpart, and the dweller in a 'favela' in Rio would be happy to have the one-room-and-kitchen flat currently being condemned and demolished in Hungary. Scott Greer observed that, by the standards of poorer countries, there is really no sub-standard American housing (1966, p. 519); in the United States a district is classified as slum if it houses two persons per room, a density only recently achieved and regarded as normal in Hungary. (In Hungary in 1968 the per-room density was 2 as compared with 2.35 in 1960 (SZOVOSZ, 1969).) Besides meaning different things in different countries, the housing problem also changes with the passage of time. In Hungary, for example, 600,000 housing units were built between 1960 and 1970 to improve the housing of the people, but there continued to be just as many complaints as before. Four hundred thousand more units were planned for the following five years, to provide new housing for a further 1.5 million people; but scarcely anybody believed that the whole fifteen-year construction programme would solve the problem. If a public opinion poll at any past or future date should ask 'What is your greatest personal or family problem?' the commonest answer would continue to be 'housing'. In the late fall of 1970 we conducted a public opinion poll at Mako (Hungary). Half of the interviewed persons admitted having problems, and 40 per cent of these cited housing as the most pressing problem, leaving far behind all other problems like health, bringing up children, material situation, job, etc., etc. It was the same with the question 'What is the most pressing problem of your city?', the answers showing even higher interest in housing. It is in a way shocking that, in an industrially undeveloped city, with poor below-standard public facilities, three times as many residents considered housing the main problem, and only a minority complained about the lack of commerce and industry. We cannot, of course, draw far-reaching conclusions from a pilot study, but we can propose hypothetically that in the majority of Hungarian cities the above formulated questions would be similarly answered. It is reasonable to conclude that the housing problem cannot be understood in any simplistic way. Both for theoretical purposes and for practical policy purposes, it has to be understood in social terms.

What then causes housing problems, and what is their social meaning and importance? There are answers of two kinds to these questions. There are those who hold that shortage is the essence of the housing problem, while others—hitherto a minority—try to explain it in relation to social structure as a problem of distribution and of social inequalities. Though shortage and distribution are certainly not independent elements of the housing problem (you cannot distribute the non-existent, many would argue), we intend to treat these two lines of argument separately, as a convenient way of looking for logical principles of housing policy.

The housing shortage

Housing policy experts in most countries have been convinced that the housing problem is caused by shortage, or more precisely by the number of dwellings classified by various indicators as sub-standard. That implies that the housing problem could be solved by building more housing, using a larger proportion of the national income. The idea is particularly appealing in socialist countries where the state largely commands the housing market, produces a large proportion of the new housing from its budget, and owns a large proportion of the national housing stock. In those conditions it is easy for experts in housing policy to assume that the solution of the housing problem depends entirely on material resources and building capacity. Certainly this view has been widely held in Hungary, by economists and even by some sociologists, as well as by journalists.

If housing shortage causes the housing problem, we may ask, next, what causes the housing shortage? To that question there are two kinds of answers: one locates the causes of the shortage outside the economy, the other cites economic causes.

Some of the causes obviously lie outside the socialist economic system. Socialist countries began by inheriting their housing stock. In 1970, more than half of the housing in Hungary had been built before the Second World War under a different social order, and the new order could not be held responsible for it. Also, quite a lot of housing had been destroyed or damaged in the war. To that extent the previous social order and the Second World War could be held responsible for the housing shortage. But with the passage of time that argument becomes less and less convincing. The Hungarian national economy has long since healed its war wounds. It could also, if desired, have rebuilt more than half of its pre-war stock by 1970, if it had elected to build at the rate planned for the decade beginning in 1970—a rate which would replace a quarter of the national housing stock in ten years. It makes less and less sense to regard the housing problem as inherited: whatever the housing problem is, it is now a product of the new regime.

As the effects of the Second World War faded, there was increasing reference to two other causes which did not arise directly from the economy. They were the acceleration of rural migration to the cities, and the demographic revolution which increased the population faster than had been expected. In Hungary the growth of population has been slower, so rural migration to the cities gets most of the blame for the housing shortage. Though there is some sharing of houses in a few villages, the main housing shortage in Hungary is undoubtedly urban. There are villages with empty houses—Gyurufu in Baranya county was completely depopulated by 1970. In the cities, responsible officials often use the mass media to protest indignantly against irresponsible rural migration—against people who leave their adequate rural homes to move to crowded sub-tenancies in urban slums, then appear as claimants for urban housing. 'Old' city-dwellers agree with the officials. Many would like to see the housing problem solved by 'repatriating the flotsam' back to their villages of origin. Nothing quite as radical as that is done, but there have been some administrative and occasionally police moves in that direction—some municipal regulations discourage movement to Budapest, others prohibit the occupation of condemned flats. The urban authorities' worries are understandable. They are upset by their failure to speed up the pace of housing construction; and at the same time the more houses they build, the more rural people migrate to the cities, and paradoxically aggravate the housing situation.

But the 'irresponsible' rural migrants have their reasons: sub-standard rural housing, inadequate public services, lack of jobs, and working prospects. To change a worse for a better way of life—in the full sense of 'way of life'—it may be worthwhile to leave good village housing, even for the worst kind of shack on the city's periphery. To the extent that economic causes prompt the migration, we cannot accept the arguments which try to ascribe the urban housing problems to causes outside the economy. In Hungary these arguments are specially inappropriate, because the migration to the cities has actually been less than notionally it ought to have been. During the fifties and sixties migration to the Hungarian cities was slower than the decrease of agricultural population, and the proportion of rural population seems now to be unexpectedly high in relation to those employed in agriculture; while only one-third of the nation's wage-earners work at country trades, more than half of the population live in country villages. The difference is accounted for by the amount of commuting from village housing to city employment, an amount which occasions some official anxiety. So the inadequate rate of housing construction is not a consequence of too much migration to the cities. It is really a cause of there being too little migration to the cities: the urban housing shortage leaves Hungary 'under-urbanized'.

It is not only in Eastern Europe that the rate of production of housing seems to lag behind other kinds of economic growth. It is worth noticing some international comparisons. Together they indicate that non-economic factors—or perhaps, defects in economic incentive—have some universal tendency to restrict the volume of housing construction to less than the level which national income might justify.

In the United States, for example, since the turn of the century the proportion of housing investment has continuously decreased in relation to total capital investments (Meyerson *et al.*, 1962), and a similar trend has occurred in other countries also. As a market economy grows, housing attracts less and less of business investment. Scientific and technological change increase the rates of return and replacement of capital investment in most sectors of the economy, but not in housing. Industrial investments may pay for themselves in five to ten years, while housing investments take twenty-five to forty years. It is understandable, therefore, that profit-motivated entrepreneurs are not much interested in housing investments, except in limited luxury markets. In developed capitalist market economies, entrepreneurs are not keen to finance cheaper housing; they contribute to the housing shortage by directing capital to the over-production of more expensive buildings. More expensive apartment buildings yield higher profits and faster capital turnover. But the relatively low and slow return from most housing investment is obviously related to the relatively slow development of building technology, and the continuing employment of costly manual methods in the labour-intensive building industry. It is not easy to know which is the cause and which the effect: whether poor profits on building investments hold back the development of building technology, or the complex nature of the industry retards the technology and therefore limits the profitability of investment. Whatever the cause, there is certainly a tendency in market economic systems which dampens business interest in housing. That tendency should warn us not to expect much success for housing policies in market economies. It will be suggested later that open markets may sometimes provide efficient supplies of housing—but in other conditions, not in capitalist economic systems.

If housing investment tends to lag behind other capital growth in market economies, what happens in socialist countries, which do not allow the same spontaneous processes, but plan their housing development deliberately within the framework of the overall national economy? However surprising the answer may seem, we believe that the difference between the treatment of housing and other investment has been even greater in the planned economies.

In the new order, socialist industrialization was seen as the most important task of economic planning. Housing expenditure was classified as unprofitable—as consumption of national income, rather than as productive investment. So it could happen that in the early 1950s the volume of housing construction fell to an absolutely minimal level; and, even when it revived in later years, the increase in construction was done more for political than for economic reasons. In Hungary we came to agree with Tibor Liska who urged a more market-oriented housing policy (Liska, 1969), because such a policy would help to remove an irrational element from the economic system, and transform the provision of housing into a more efficient and economical operation. It should be emphasized, nevertheless, that market methods could only be applied in restricted ways and with limited benefits, because the problems described above occur even in the purest market economies.

Some researchers explain the relative decrease of housing investment as a direct effect of rising income. Louis Winnick (1955), for example, states that demand for housing occupies a low place in the order of general consumer demands. He examined family budgets (Maisel and Winnick, 1966), and found that, although expenditure on housing increased with income, it did not increase proportionately, so, as income increased, a declining proportion of it was spent on housing. There may be various reasons for that. People may have as much housing as they want. A. Baranov (1969), in analysing the level of satisfaction with housing, believes that housing needs and demands are not unlimited, and may be saturated at a relatively modest level. But, if Baranov is right, there should be some level of income at which the declining demand is easily met, there is no more housing shortage, and the housing problem is absolutely solved. But not even in America or Sweden does that appear to happen. The proportion of housing expenditure in the general family budget seems to be determined by the pressure of other demands on the budget, as well as by housing need: the declining demand for more housing may not necessarily signify satisfaction.

For similar reasons it is hard to accept the argument that the housing shortage is mainly a consequence of unbalance between demand and supply. Liska (1969) argued that in Hungary the housing shortage was caused by artificially depressed levels of rent. He thought that the unrealistically low rents of some types of housing increased demand, and that the market would balance, and the excess demand would disappear, if all rents were raised to market levels. Besides 'clearing the market' he also thought that market rents would stimulate housing construction. Liska's arguments deserve attention, and his proposition that the housing problem depends on the functioning of the housing economy as a whole, and not just on the volume of construction, is especially fruitful. But it is difficult to accept his hypothesis about the role of market balance in solving social problems and conflicts, because the hypothesis was derived from one sector only of the market—the state-owned rental sector. Hungary still has a large open housing market, with genuine market prices, in which anyone can buy a family house or a flat for life, if he can pay the price. But shortages and resentments continue, among the many who do feel a desire for better housing but cannot afford the market prices. They may suffer real social disadvantage as a result, and feelings of dissatisfaction and injustice.

In order to understand the housing problem properly it is necessary to set aside the explanations which ascribe the problem to the housing shortage, and its various possible causes. It is specially important to progress beyond these 'shortage' explanations because, in the world of policy, they tend to be self-frustrating. As often as one expert group proposes to solve the housing problem by increasing the rate of housing construction, other expert groups will demonstrate that the national economy cannot afford to divert further resources to construction.

What is really needed, to understand the problem and to meet it with effective policy-making, is a social view of housing which perceives it as part of the whole social system of income distribution and social reward. We must examine the housing problem as part of the general social structure, with all its tensions and conflicting interests.

Social components of the housing problem

As suggested earlier, we have to discover the place of housing in the systems of social distribution and reward if we wish to understand how housing becomes a social problem. Not all scarcities turn into 'social problems'. We do not talk of a 'car problem' because everybody does not have a car, or because those with higher incomes can buy bigger cars than those with lower incomes. Different capacities to buy particular goods are regarded as natural in a structured society. If housing differences, and differences in access to housing, do nevertheless get defined as a social problem, that measures the special importance which is accorded to housing in both capitalist and industrialized socialist societies, as an element in the system of social rewards. Scott Greer writes very convincingly: 'The housing situation turns into a problem if many think that housing is unjustly distributed. If somebody regards his housing situation as a social reward, if somebody regards himself as a hard-working, honest citizen worthy of recognition in all other spheres of activity, but still cannot obtain adequate housing, then he feels cheated.' (1966, p. 519.) We probably do not misinterpret this statement if we conclude that those who are dissatisfied with their housing situation feel cheated because of the unwarrantedly big difference between their own and others' housing, and because the differences signify altogether too much social inequality. Edith Elmer Wood, one of the earliest critics of American social housing policy, stated as early as 1934 that social inequalities were the cause of the housing problem. She wrote:

The housing problem is unavoidably associated with modern industrial civilization and cannot be solved independently. *The play of demand and supply does not offer a solution because the unbalance between income distribution and building costs excludes two-thirds of the population from effective demand for new housing.* Though some of the old housing is acceptable, most of it is in shocking condition. (1934, p. 137; author's emphasis.)

Differences in housing situation and in the capacity to acquire housing reflect more general social inequalities and conflicts—but also help to cause them, as the housing system in its turn affects the social structure and becomes a factor in keeping it open or rigid. When Scott Greer (1966) writes that 'many complain of the unjust distribution of housing . . .', he refers to the open, conscious voicing of the real situation.

It seems obvious that housing conditions can affect individual and social life. The nature and location of people's housing can—at least to some degree—influence their social relationships, their job-getting and performance at work, and even their children's school results. Scott Greer sees a vicious circle in this mutual relationship of housing and social structure. If he is right, then, if society stamps somebody as less important and useful, that person will be provided with poorer housing; the poor housing will reduce his social opportunities; his job performance will deteriorate; so will his children's school results. As he and his family produce less and less, society will give them less and less rewards. Gypsy children living in miserable makeshift hovels have no room to do their school homework; most of them cannot finish basic schooling—so cannot get worthwhile jobs, so continue their degrading way of life, bringing up their children in turn in the same miserable makeshift hovels.

The functioning of the housing system thus becomes a social problem if it contributes to the perpetuation of social privileges and social disadvantages. (See Pahl, 1968), for a similar formation.) Thus we arrive at the sociological principle of any kind of social policy.

Wherever vicious circles occur, there should be public intervention to break them. It may often be necessary to intervene at a number of points in the circle of causation. If the housing system is acting as a link or component of such a circle, it may be necessary to intervene in housing, as well as at other points in the circle. Only in this sense will we argue that the housing problem arises from housing policy, and within that policy especially from the system of distributing housing in conditions of housing shortage. But, however general its causes, the housing problem will certainly surface, and appear to people, as a housing shortage. To break the vicious circle, it may well be necessary among other things to provide more housing. But it matters at least as much what kinds of houses are built, and who gets them. Merely to build more is not yet social policy. It is quite possible for increased construction, if ill-directed, to intensify the vicious circle (though this is usually prevented by the process of filtering to be described later), and so to aggravate the housing problem. A housing policy deserves the

name only if it goes beyond questions of construction to ensure
that the housing system as a whole does not contribute to the
accumulation of social disadvantages, or reduce social mobility.
Does that general description of the housing problem fit the
particular housing problems of the socialist countries, including
Hungary? Is housing a social problem in Eastern Europe, or is
there merely a housing shortage?

It would be a grave mistake to apply the formulations of
western sociology in any mechanical way to East European
conditions. Housing policies in socialist countries have basically different foundations from those of capitalist countries.
Therefore, before analysing the working of the Hungarian
national system, we must first discuss the underlying ideologies
of housing and architectural policy. A careful analysis of these
ideologies may suggest that the housing problems arise from the
system of housing economics, and not from any lack of good
intentions to provide more housing.

Ideologies of housing and architectural policy

How far should the state intervene in the production and distribution of housing, and how far should this intervention go in
socialist states?

In Hungary the guiding principles of housing policy are two:
housing should be a universal provision, not a market commodity; and its production and distribution should not be a means
of unearned income. In the early centralist and bureaucratic
years of the new regime the state took over the ownership and
distribution of all significant income-earning holdings of
housing, including apartment buildings. It established a monopoly of large-scale building, including the construction of urban
apartment buildings. It thus assumed general responsibility for
meeting the housing needs of the society.

Capitalist production and marketing of housing ceased.
People could still buy, sell, or exchange their own private
houses; they could barter house for house with the state distri-
butors of housing; in some conditions they could buy new
housing from the state builders; and they could co-operate and
barter with one another to build houses for themselves. Despite
those continuing private opportunities it was the state that had
assumed the fundamental responsibility for meeting the

people's housing needs, including the backlog of demand that had accumulated during the war years. The bulk of the housing need was real enough. Nevertheless it was no longer 'effective demand' as understood and limited in market conditions. It had become a universal right, a demand sanctioned by the socialist state itself. That strengthened the demand, and the rate of growth of population and new households strengthened it further.

With limited housing stock and limited building capacity, the new authorities began by trying to improve the distribution of existing accommodation. Inevitably—since they had to apply egalitarian principles and try to liquidate existing housing inequalities—that included some forced sharing of houses, by co-tenancies. Those created so much social tension that the authorities were soon forced to declare them a strictly temporary expedient. Tolerance of co-tenancy depends on the custom of the country. Where it has been customary for several generations or family branches to share housing, such sharing has been a viable socialist policy, as for a long time in the USSR and Bulgaria. But, where industrial society has created a general expectation and practice of 'one house, one family', as in urban Hungary, people put high value on that arrangement and the demand for it is tenacious.

The other partial solution consisted in the removal of arbitrarily selected members of the former ruling classes. A certain amount of good housing became vacant in this way, and the good units were mainly occupied by the leading functionaries of the new socialist state. There was thus a change of tenants in the best units of housing and in the best districts. But the difference between tbe best and the worst housing remained, and so did the inequalities between their respective tenants. The officially-directed changes of tenancy eventually ceased.

By the mid-1950s it had become an accepted principle that social inequalities in housing could not be eradicated by re-distributing the existing housing stock. Equality could only be achieved by demolishing a great many old sub-standard houses and constructing a great many new ones. Housing units are so expensive, durable, comparatively indivisible, and fixed in particular neighbourhoods, that consumer equality is harder to achieve in housing than in any other sphere of distribution. But at the same time it has been proven beyond serious doubt that the home is the centre and organizing frame of the family's consumer status, its general behaviour, and its aspirations. It follows that persisting inequalities in housing will have the effect of perpetuating other consumer inequalities between the strata of society. In this sense housing arrangements, and housing policies designed to affect the housing system, cannot avoid having a wider socio-political significance of a distinctive kind.

Because comparatively little could be achieved by redistributing the existing stock, we believed that equality between residents could only be achieved by a faster rate of building, to higher standards, with standardized housing forms and facilities. That required, above all, a huge volume of building. But that was not what the state was providing. Though there are no satisfactory statistics, it is clear that between 1950 and 1955 the rate of housing construction fell below the levels of the 1940s, 1930s, and even the 1920s.

That surprising decline in construction was a deliberate part of economic policy. The national economic policy of those early revolutionary years was committed to forcing extensive and rapid industrialization without an adequate labour force, without export capacity, and with a production system which was all too often indifferent to quality or saleability. The means included export of agricultural output, and severe restriction of the volume of consumer goods. To allocate resources to housing seemed at that time, to those policy-makers, like eating the original egg before it had hatched the magic goose that would one day lay the golden eggs. It seemed anti-social as well as shortsighted: like other consumer goods, housing seemed to cater only for selfish individual interests. Such interests must be subordinated, for many years to come, to the requirements of an imaginative and constructive programme of heavy industrial development, which would serve the long-term economic interests of the whole society.

Underlying those practical priorities was a strangely self-defeating article of faith. Ideological considerations caused a paradoxical change of policy in the evaluation of housing investments within the general framework of the economy. Precisely because housing was singled out as a specially important consumer good, it came to be starved of resources.

This paradox is best explained by an example. As long as basic needs for food were satisfied, no special importance was ever given to the supply of other consumer goods. Shoes, radios, furniture, liquor, and other 'unnecessaries' were of interest only to the consumers themselves; they were not essential means of production, or of economic growth. Even when the production of such consumer goods lagged far behind the production of capital goods, that was perceived as a cause of personal hardship, but not economic imbalance or inefficiency. Nor were consumer goods of that kind so essential to personal survival that they needed special administrative distribution. They were not like food in times of famine. Nobody ever thought of shoes as peoples' birthright. So nobody ever dreamed of removing shoes from commerce and charging the urban and rural councils with their distribution, using criteria of need, or perhaps of social merit and trustworthiness. Shoes remained ordinary market merchandise even under socialism. They were for buying and selling, not for satisfying fundamental needs; if a deficient and inflationary economy could supply only ill-designed and poorly-made shoes to the market, that was still no cause for socialist intervention. Even children's shoes continued to be treated as market goods—though their prices were restrained by some subsidy. For the benefit of families with children, they continued to be available as market goods at prices which varied with quality; so all that was needed to acquire shoes was money, without any need for bureaucratic intervention.

Because shoes were market goods, they were economic goods in a broader sense. They took their share of consumer spending; shortages or over-supplies would have predictable economic effects, and would concern the economic planners accordingly. It also followed that nobody need lose money by producing them—they would sell at prices which would eventually return the capital and costs of producing them. But housing was different. It was so essential, and met such basic human needs, that it had been removed from the open market, to be allocated to need and merit by administrative processes instead of market processes, at low rents which bore no relation to production costs. It followed that housing was not an economic commodity in the same, broad sense as shoes. In relation to its real cost, housing took negligible proportions of consumer spending. It would continue to take negligible proportions, however large or small were the resources allocated to producing it.

The consequence was that economists and policy-makers ceased to regard housing as a useful economic commodity. Production of shoes continued to be functional, production of housing was stamped non-functional. Production of shoes signified economic growth, production of housing signified a concession to political necessity. The political pressure was considerable. Indeed the housing shortage was so unpopular that all sorts of excuses were invented for it. It was variously blamed on subjective errors by successive leaderships, technical backwardness or technical mistakes in the building industry, shortage of material resources, etc. But the brutal truth is that the steep decline of Hungarian state housing construction, to a record 'low' of 20 to 25,000 units per year, was quite deliberate: these were the planned volumes through those years. The volume had been decimated because housing had first been defined as a consumer commodity, but had then been removed from market distribution, and distributed instead at such artificially low rents that it became the most unprofitable of all consumer commodities to produce. Economic planners saw housing investment as 'returnless expenditure', a necessary evil to be minimized as far as possible.

Through the 1960s similar conditions and beliefs prevailed in most socialist countries. There was a relatively slow increase in housing production, and it represented a continuously declining proportion of total investment. This was enforced despite rising productivity and evidence of increasing housing needs, and despite the fact that there was no saturated demand in any of these socialist states.

In the 1970s housing construction still competed poorly for resources. Industrial and other capital investment was the business of powerful big institutions, trusts, and central-government ministries. They tended to be much more influential than the local agencies responsible for housing. The hierarchy of power and economic responsibility put local government at the bottom; the housing for which local agencies was responsible suffered from the theoretical definitions indicated above; and there were no effective channels of consumer influence on economic policy. So what happened in practice, in the competition for capital resources, was that local council officials representing housing needs were confronted by general directors of trusts in charge of huge capital movements, who usually won easily. Industry won over construction; and within the allocations to construction, other kinds of building won against housing. Industrial plans were typically detailed and executed by industrial and construction authorities. They typically allocated the least possible share of their resources to housing the intended work-force, and less still to housing anyone else. Their conception of social needs was expressed in the construction of mass assembly halls. Their inventive architectural designers delighted in creating factory structures like cathedrals, often to house mediocre technological equipment. Thus industry itself grew hungrier for whatever construction capacity existed. So did the bureaucracy, with its burgeoning ambitions to administer business and government from grander, even more expensive office premises. So the monumental industrial constructions at the outskirts of cities were matched by monumental official buildings at their centres. This redirection of resources from housing to industrial and bureaucratic construction was made even easier by the organizational association of the building authorities and the building enterprises.

What are the consequences of all this for the consumer? If housing is not a consumer commodity of a market kind, but not productive socialist investment either—so that the state production of housing is therefore a matter of welfare or social policy—how will the consumers fare, and what will happen to their earlier housing inequalities?

In the sphere of private consumption—excepting some services like education, recreation, health care—only housing was accorded special status and taken off the market for administrative distribution, with the greatest possible equality in housing for all members of society as the most important goal of social policy. Rents were set low, and the same for all. This was for a long time one of the showpieces of socialist consumer policy. The low rents were enjoyed by all who already had adequate housing, or were allocated it. Meanwhile families who did not have any housing, or who wished to change from inadequate quarters or inconvenient addresses, joined the mounting numbers on the waiting lists for state housing, without much early hope of getting it, or therefore of getting the low rents and high housing standards of their more fortunate brethren.

That traditional vertical inequality was soon accompanied by specific horizontal inequalities. Among people within similar social categories there were the elderly who had homes, and the young who did not have them yet; there were the original urban residents with homes and the newer immigrants without them; there were fortunate families with official connections and unfortunate families with none. Among people of the same income, working together in the same workshop or office, there would commonly be tenants, sub-tenants, bed-tenants, and boarders in workers' hostels—and the lucky tenants of whole houses or apartments were privileged like princes. Privileged housing carried with it an almost feudal distinction. To receive it was to stride eight or ten years ahead along the road to consumer security, because the average value of the 'free' state housing unit was about eight years' income of a worker. Between workers earning 25,000 forints of Hungarian currency a year (early 1970s), one might thus be given housing worth 200,000 forints while another got nothing. In one of the greatest ironies of the new regime, all this necessarily followed from the nature of distribution in kind. Because housing is indivisible, one family receives an ample amount of it and another receives nothing. Because housing is costly and its production is limited, and because everybody has a right to it, the number of entitled claimants surpasses many times the number of available units.

This competitive situation, with perverse effects and grotesque social inequalities, tends to characterize all such distributions in kind of basic, high-value necessities. The horizontal inequalities soon generate vertical ones. Some families are better able than others to exert pressure on the distributing authorities. The distributing authorities work in an atmosphere in which they and others—technocrats, intellectual élites—are developing and competing for position in a new ruling hierarchy of power, income, and prestige. Families low in the hierarchy have less chance in the competition for housing; families without acceptable housing are handicapped in the competition to climb the hierarchy. Housing allocations do not go to correct other inequalities, they tend to reinforce them. This is understandable: when everyone is equally entitled to 'free goods' there are no clear official criteria for allocating the inadequate supplies of them.

In the first years of socialist construction, after the initial revolutionary changes, the ideological atmosphere encouraged the assumption that substantial equality had been achieved. If so, there should really be no further need for social policy: in a society in which even relative poverty had no place, it became unthinkable to suggest that any particular social class was unequal enough to need special state assistance, in housing or anything else. Through these years the very heart of politics was social policy: the realization of just, social relationships based on equality.

Thus housing policy came to be equated with social housing policy. It would have been considered malicious nonsense to differentiate between the two in the atmosphere of official optimism of those times. It would have been unthinkable to propose different housing arrangements for different social classes—there *were* no different social classes! To avoid any such discrimination it followed that, for two decades, the limited supplies of free socialist housing were distributed without any official requirement that they go to people with lower incomes or larger needs. Basically all Hungarian citizens irrespective of their position or income were entitled to free housing, and the quality of the free housing compared favourably with the best existing housing. This state of affairs produced a general euphoria about socialist housing policy. Housing production was determined by general political and economic considerations, and houses were designed without specific knowledge about their future tenants. One thing was certain: the tenant families would be members of the new society, equally entitled without reference to any social differences between them. The size and age and sex structure of families were the only accepted criteria. These idealist illusions were readily accepted and embraced by the architects and builders, who proceeded to design standardized accommodations for the average household.

So there were standard designs for the standard entitlements of standard families. The question of standards is important in the relationship between society and its building industries, and it leads us to the question of needs and requirements. The question is important everywhere, not only in socialist countries. Wherever, by the adoption of large-scale industrial methods, the direct relationship between the architect and his 'consumer' is broken, the social aim of architectural design becomes problematic.

In a complex, industrial, and urbanized society the conflict between the technical and human sides of architecture may be polarized in many ways. In this technological century, architecture has at its disposal a vastly enriched armoury of new technical possibilities. New materials and revolutionary methods enable the architect to realize his boldest dreams. This new era of architecture brought important changes in quantity production. It shortened building time and increased building capacity. But, paradoxically, the increase of technical capacity was associated with increasing uncertainty about the human interests involved. Today's architect can produce more and more work which differs from the traditional and the customary, but he has less and less certainty that he can discover what is actually needed. One effect of these uncertainties has been to prompt architects to turn with new interest to sciences, sociology among them, which may provide scientific information about social needs.

The resort to the social sciences is new. The need for it is new—it is only recently that the designer ceased to deal directly with the client who would occupy the building. Before the change, for thousands of years, the builder knew the customer and built for his known needs. Since the change, the builder rarely knows who the occupiers will actually be. The same change had come earlier in most other industries: with the development of the capitalist market economy, the shoemaker, the joiner, the tailor had had to learn how to produce for a market without advance knowledge of the potential customers and their continuously changing demands. They learned how to adapt their supplies to the market responses. When people tired of one style of shoe, they could soon enough supply another style. But the problem for the architect and builder is incomparably more difficult. The essence of the difficulty is that the product may well endure for a century or more. It will have to satisfy the needs of two or three or four generations of people who are not yet born, in a world in which the pace of social change is accelerating.

Other causes have joined in separating the building designer from direct acquaintance with the customers and their interests. The world has come to understand the extraordinary social responsibility that goes with building planning and design. So all advanced countries, whatever their social systems, have developed extensive public interference in the market concerned. Governments regulate the development and subdivision of land, the layout of neighbourhoods, the standard and design of buildings, and even their permitted uses and rents. This public control of physical development has become specially important in socialist countries where significant proportions of land and building development have been taken out of the market system altogether. That change actually enlarges the architects' freedom. With no market to follow, they can more freely express their own ideas. They are not only freer to build whatever they like; the work is often freer from criticism or 'feedback' from the users of the fabric. There is no market mechanism, either to express the customers' judgements and preferences, or to provide a basis for other judgements of the economy and value, or the success or failure, of the product.

This increased freedom helped to create and develop the frightening phantom of the average standard person. If he is left without any market or other 'feedback' from the customers, the architect necessarily has to look for rule-of-thumb norms and standards to guide his work. When the tailors and shoemakers and carpenters faced the same problem, as mentioned above, they got more help from market mechanisms; but the standards which they developed could mostly also be related clearly enough to the biological nature of man. Between them the facts of human biology, and the technical possibilities of the industry, could resolve most problems of standardization. For the architect who had to think a hundred years ahead, the biological basis had the special attraction that it was unlikely to change from generation to generation. So it was fatally easy to conceive the idea of the 'standard human being' whose biology allowed the specification of standard characteristics and needs. And the idea got special encouragement from the political climate of the socialist states. In any egalitarian, democratically-minded society, decent living conditions are properly regarded as a universal natural right. If spontaneous social processes do not assure this right—and they were not doing so in Eastern Europe —society must obviously intervene to correct the situation. For that purpose it is first necessary to define what are to be regarded as decent living conditions, which in turn requires definition of the general social needs to be satisfied by the built environment. In an equal society, those needs must presumably be defined as the same for all.

Meanwhile the technical development of the building industry contributed its share to the emergence of the standard human being. The mechanization of the industry included much standardization of building machinery and tools. Building with bigger prefabricated components called for bigger transporters and cranes, with more and more constraints on the sites where they could be used. There was increasing standardization of the interiors, exteriors, and locations of new construction.

Despite all these reasons for inventing him, the standardized human being proved to be a phantom.

The new East European societies are still, to a considerable degree, differentiated societies. They are segmented both vertically and horizontally, and the segments are penetrated through and through by complex webs of various hierarchies. At the present stage of technical development, division of labour, socialist property relationships, the society values and rewards its members in a number of ways. The groups or classes formed by these divisions of labour and reward develop differing modes of behaviour, follow differing values and norms, and have unavoidably different needs. People's positions in the system of social stratification do much to determine their ways of life. The society is sufficiently differentiated and complex to generate a considerable diversity of ways of life, and a corresponding diversity of needs to be satisfied by housing and urban design.

One decisive component of the way of life, the particular 'basket' of goods and services consumed by any particular household, is heavily affected by the household's position in the system of social stratification. The level of income is the best indicator of status. In limiting what the family can spend it does a good deal to affect their spending priorities, including the housing they can afford, and the equipment and services that will go with their housing. Those in turn may determine which housekeeping functions will be done at home by some groups, while appearing as service requirements for others. Those and other details of the pattern of consumption affect the amount of time spent at home, and how it is spent. Groups with different income and education use their homes in widely differing ways, and their functional needs differ accordingly.

What holds for families holds also for the members within them. The roles of spouses, parents, and children vary with social and economic circumstances, and so do their housing needs. How much privacy do individual members of the family need? How much independence do the children want? Which households therefore want many partitioned spaces, which want a few large spaces, in their houses? And so on. If the designer's task is to create functional spaces, he has to know what particular pattern of functional needs to expect.

But it is not enough that design should be well adapted to functional needs. Unavoidably, housing design creates or influences demands, as well as satisfying them. This happens because, in addition to its functional performance, housing is also a very important form and symbol of social reward. It may often be the most substantial and showy proof of the family's social standing. That may be more significant than ever in industrialized and urbanized societies in which other signals—like dress, speech, manners—lose some of their significance as social indicators. It is not every family that puts great importance on its housing as a status symbol; but, in so far as many families do so, that in itself may alter both their spending priorities and their housing priorities. They may subordinate other, more functional needs to the desire—a subjective desire based nevertheless on objective social observation—for more impressive-looking housing. It is at this point that the symbols available—the range and styles of housing available—become important, and are apt to be determined as much by the design professions as by the market. Superficially it may appear possible to solve these problems in a market way, letting each family decide how much of its income to spend on getting how much of what type of housing. But that does not offer a satisfactory solution in the long run, because houses outlast those for whom they are built, and also because status-seekers can only respond to the options they are offered. If I want a house to eat and sleep in, I may be able to specify the functional house that I need. But if I want a house as a social reward and status symbol, what I need is something relative, determined by the hierarchy of options available, and the status that is thought to attach to each option. The whole pattern of options, and the status-inequalities ascribed to it, do not amount to something that anyone can demand in a market way. But they represent inequalities which socialist states cannot be expected to embrace officially. Hence, again, the idea that all new housing should be designed identically for equal people. But that idea encounters the three contradictions already noticed: people are not quite equal in any society; even when they are, they have diverse housing needs; and houses built now must outlast by some generations the needs for which they are designed.

If architects nevertheless persist in trying to operate with the phantom of the standard human being, it becomes necessary to give substance to the phantom. Some group of officials must determine actual needs and standards. Officialdom will characteristically define its own needs, and its own desired standards, and generalize those. The standard housing that is then built will accordingly neglect the need of other groups, to their disadvantage. In that way, strictly standardized design may well do more to confirm or increase existing inequalities than to reduce them.

There is, thus, a dilemma. *Architecture which does not differentiate to the extent required by social differences may contribute to increasing those differences.* But architecture does not merely respond to social needs, it also helps to mould them. So if present needs reflect an undesirable range of existing social differences, then *architecture which does differentiate to the extent required by social differences may help to perpetuate the differences.*

Faced with that dilemma, how can present-day analysis of the structure of society contribute usefully to its transformation?

Current analysis can be the basis of some prognostication. The methods of prognostication are not well developed, but they are better than nothing. Some trends can be projected with reasonable confidence. If we assume a certain rhythm of economic growth, we can deduce the likely evolution of the society's occupational structure, the changes that structure may bring about in educational standards, and some effects of rising income. On that basis it may be possible to pose some social alternatives in patterns of consumption and life-style.

Urban planners and designers can expect to accelerate or

retard some of those developments, and influence some of the social choices, through the social effects of their current planning and design. But they should not decide what kinds of behaviour the built environment ought to facilitate, and what kinds it ought to repress, without clear assumptions about the basic values of human life. By that proviso, we concede that the designer's duty is a scientific, direction-finding duty. It could perhaps be called a meta-scientific or ideological duty, but only in a certain sense and to a certain extent. The value-choices for the future must conform with practical possibilities derived from today's actual situations, if we wish to prevent the rebirth of an ideological phantom of the standard human being.

Turning back to our opening argument, we can now say: *the architect can assert his freedom only if he does so, not in order to evade reality, but in order to transform it on the basis of real knowledge.* In this task the relation of design to social knowledge is not unlike its relation to technical knowledge. The possibilities and limits in the uses of concrete or glass are to be found in the nature of concrete and glass, and to exploit their possibilities requires experts to know their limits. *To shape society by architectural means requires a similar basis of social knowledge.* We support the idea that society should be moulded by architects using knowledge derived from the social sciences, against the idea that it should be moulded by technocrats, using the phantom of the standard human being.

In Hungary, housing policy sought to break into the circular problems of housing and architecture by removing housing from the market, and inventing the convenient phantom of the standard human being. The attempt was substantially unsuccessful. In face of the differentiated housing needs of the society, and the persisting presence of a good deal of market behaviour outside the state housing sector, it did not prove possible to equalize everybody's housing conditions by resort to administrative distribution of housing, and a uniform standard in all housing construction. The poor performance of those policies arose partly also because they were often diverted from 'pure' housing purposes to give priority to the purpose of forced industrialization.

Earlier researches into the sociology of settlement in Hungary and in other socialist countries (Szelenyi and Konrad, 1969; Zivkovic, 1968; Duric, 1969; Musil, n.d; L. Macková,

1970 and 1971) had proved that housing never entirely lost its market character, and that differences between households, both in their actual housing and in their chances of acquiring any desired kind of housing, including housing of good quality, continued to depend on their social status. For this reason we decided that, in our research into urban and housing sociology at Pecs and Szeged in Hungary, we would methodically map the working of the housing system, so as to discover what chances various social strata had of acquiring various kinds of housing, and what effects the various kinds of housing appeared to have on the households' fortunes: in short, we would study both halves of the 'magic circle'. The following chapter will report what we found.

CHAPTER 2

Structure and Functioning of the Socialist Housing System: The Hungarian Case

Housing mobility within the state and market sector of the housing economy

IT IS a truism that richer people usually have better homes. Housing is the most important consumer commodity in every modern society, and it is unequally available to different social strata just as other consumer commodities are. That much is obvious. The subject only becomes sociologically interesting if we do not limit ourselves to the static description of the diversity or inequality of housing conditions, but try to reveal the dynamics of the system of distribution.

Housing stock is increasing in every industrially developed country, though the pace of increase varies. If supply expands, the various strata of society may improve their housing situation. But it does not follow automatically that they will all gain, or all at the same rate; in some circumstances some groups may even lose, relatively or absolutely. The sociologist should be interested, therefore, to know how the quantitative increase and qualitative differentiation of the whole housing stock affects the housing situation of different social strata, and whether it narrows or widens inequalities between the extremes of income and status.

The concept of filtering was evolved by housing economists (see Ratcliff, 1945 and 1949; Fischer and Winnick, 1951; and Grigsby, 1963), but surprisingly enough it was neglected by sociologists. People 'filter' up or down to relatively better or worse housing; particular types of housing 'filter' up or (more commonly) down from one social class of occupiers to another. Thus the once-best houses will filter downwards if even better houses are added to the stock, as the richest people who want the best move house from the old best to the new best. If housing specialists are interested in how the houses filter, sociologists are more interested in the other side of the process: how social groups and strata change their positions within the housing system. We call this movement within the system 'housing mobility'.

But in examining housing mobility it is clearly not sufficient to consider only the qualitative differentiation of the housing stock. We will call somebody mobile if he changes his position within the housing system, and this can happen without any change in the quality of his housing. It can happen, for example, if someone moves out of an apartment with two rooms and full facilities which he merely rents, into an identical apartment with two rooms and full facilities which he owns for life. His change of tenure has changed his position in the housing system.

Position in the housing system can be described in terms of 'housing class', a concept developed a few years ago by Rex (1968) and further by Pahl (1970, pp. 53–68). To arrive at housing class, Rex used Max Weber's concept of class. In Weber's language, class need not necessarily be determined by people's relations to the system of production, e.g. as owners of the means of production, or wage-earners selling their labour. It is possible for any common economic interest to make a class, if it gives a group of people similar market situations and similar market interests. In that general sense Rex argues that we can talk of the class of home owners as against the class of tenants. Housing class is not a proper Marxist social class, but it is a very useful term in the analysis of housing systems.

We can begin by accepting that a housing system is healthy if all social groups are able to improve their housing situation, while at the same time their upward mobility does not increase the inequalities between them.

In capitalist market economies this requirement can only be realized if inequalities of income are not increasing, and if the various social strata strive equally for the improvement of their housing situation. If these two conditions are present, it should be automatic that the social strata will filter upward through the housing classes at equivalent rates, with house rents and prices proportional to housing quality functioning as regulating mechanisms.

Those simple requirements do not usually prevail in today's capitalism. The pattern of changing incomes is complex, and there are diverse class attitudes to the importance of housing. It has become necessary for social and political reasons to introduce some equalizing mechanisms into the economics of housing. These mechanisms operate partly within the market system and partly outside it, by supplementing the rental payments of low-income families, regulating private rents, or providing public housing at fixed rents.

In Hungary, and generally in East European socialist countries, the social and economic system of housing is entirely different from that capitalist model. As it developed in the late 1940s, the socialist system was based on these principles: housing should not be market merchandise; therefore its rents need not necessarily be strictly related to housing quality; rent should be a very modest item of household expenditure; within the limits of economic growth, families should have a natural right to healthy, modern, self-contained, housing, and they should receive it as distribution in kind, independent of their rent-paying capacities.

This model was designed to assure faster upward mobility for low-income strata. It was intended to achieve housing equality within the foreseeable future, or at least to reduce substantially the existent housing differences.

It was generally accepted that large-scale industrial production would replace small workshop production, and that state ownership of property would replace private ownership of it. As a logical consequence, it seemed to follow that private building and ownership of housing should represent a dwindling sector of the whole housing business.

That expectation was not fulfilled. Through the 1960s there was a steady increase in the proportion of housing construction that was wholly private, or done privately with some state subsidy. Meanwhile the number of homes built each year by the state did not increase, despite the development of industrial building technology, and the commissioning of new factories for the mass production of housing. The static state-built output was a falling proportion of the total volume of housing construction. The state output fell so far short of satisfying the society's housing needs that there was a steady increase in private housing construction, in town as well as country.

Thus, from the second half of the 1950s, most of the new socialist countries developed housing systems which differed substantially from one another in detail, but had broad similarities in principle. In the common system which emerged, there are three basic types of housing. There are state-owned rental flats, built wholly with state investment and distributed free of any capital payment. There are co-operative housing groups, which get part of their finance directly from the state, and the remainder in the form of long-term, low-interest credit supplied by the state to owners or renters. And there is private housing, built with private savings often supplemented by private, repayable bank loans. In many of the socialist countries, lately including Hungary, state industrial and commercial enterprises play an important role by helping their employees to acquire private housing. In Czechoslovakia, for example, there has been a steady increase in this type of housing aid since 1968, as shown in Table 2.1.

TABLE 2.1
Housing aid in Czechoslovakia since 1968

Year	Total number of constructed units	Number of houses built with help from state enterprises
1966	75,526	166
1967	79,297	630
1968	86,571	3,204
1969	85,659	14,164
1970	112,135	19,639

(Source: *Statisticka rocenka CSSR*, 1970, page 204; 1971, page 217.)

There are now, therefore, four suppliers of housing finance: state housing authorities, state industries, banks, and private savings. It is evident that the comparative value of these four sources for the consumers can be graded according to the amount of state subsidy that they include—an amount which varies from the whole capital cost of the house, through some of it, to none at all. Those who receive housing free of capital payment, often at low or merely nominal rents, can spend all their savings on furnishings; those who receive partly free housing have to wait for some years to call the home their own; those who build or buy without any help at all have to forfeit all their effort and savings for many years to come. Thus are the three groups formed: the privileged, the partly privileged, and the unprivileged. So the question arises whether these housing privileges are distributed to redress inequalities arising from other causes, especially income, or, on the contrary, to reinforce or increase them?

As a result of the developments described above, the housing system as a whole consists of two sectors. The state sector, in which houses are allocated to tenants by administrative action, consists of the free state housing, state housing sold on very favourable credit terms, and partly-subsidized co-operative housing. The remaining types of housing constitute what may be called a market sector, as long as it is understood that its market mechanisms are limited in various respects. We can assume that both sectors allow some forms of housing mobility. The main task of our sociological examination of the housing system is therefore to discover what kind of mobility, for which groups in society, is facilitated by each sector and by any interplay between the sectors.

First, how effective was the administrative distribution of housing within the state sector, in its professed intention to distribute housing more equally than before? Which social strata drew most advantages from the various measures of state subsidy, and how did that distribution of subsidies affect the distribution of the national income? In this chapter we will look for an answer to these questions.

There was some discussion earlier of the conditions which affect the quality of housing which different social strata want, and (which may not be the same thing) the quality which they get. If there is a general increase in the supply of housing it is to be expected that various social groups will want a share of the increase. If the general increase is to improve equalities, the groups with least income and the poorest housing must demand and get a faster improvement of their housing than anyone else gets. Our sociological study may therefore begin by asking how the housing claims which are made by different social strata relate to their actual housing situation. There would appear to be three basic possibilities:

1. Every social stratum increases its claim for housing according to its existing housing situation, so that all claims increase proportionately to the existing distribution of

housing—and, if all the claims were met, the proportionate distribution would be unchanged.

2. The claims of the lower social strata increase faster than the rest—so that, if all claims were met, there would be greater housing equality.

3. The claims of the higher social strata increase faster than the rest—so that, if all claims were met, there would be greater inequality than before.

Which of those tendencies will prevail in which conditions? We may begin by putting that particular question into the context of some more general knowledge of consumer behaviour. In any society, at the level of consumption changes with economic growth, *different sectors of consumption come to the fore*. The range of consumer goods which is most valued at a particular stage of growth tends to have an organizing effect on the whole pattern of consumption, with significant effects on modes of family life. Housing acquires that sort of special value, and organizing character, at certain levels of economic development. It does so in two related conditions: at a certain level of development for the society as a whole, but also at a certain level of development for each class within the society. So it does not necessarily happen that all classes put the same value on improving their housing situation, or increase their housing claims at the same time or at the same rate. It may happen that some strata are still too poor to regard better housing as their first priority; others have satisfied their primary housing needs, so they also have very moderate claims for more housing; while others again are at critical levels of development or income at which housing is their dominant problem, and they see a radical improvement of their housing as their most urgent need. These last may include groups who attribute exaggerated importance to their housing because they see an oppressive discrepancy between their social position and income and their housing situation—i.e. a contradiction between their social class and their housing class. In investigating the sociology of housing it may therefore be important to recognize the occupational groups for whom housing becomes an impatiently desired status symbol, because it is from them that the most explosive increase in demand for housing quality is to be expected.

We will therefore resume our questions in the following way:

1. What is the structural relation between the state sector and the market sector? Which social strata are unable to obtain free or heavily subsidized housing from the state sector, and have to satisfy their needs in the market sector, paying all or most of their housing costs themselves?
2. To what extent has the administrative distribution of state housing reduced housing inequalities between social strata? Which groups demand most housing improvement, and which groups get most improvement, from each sector?

To be able to analyse the social processes in each housing sector, we must first group the various types of housing available in each sector into the 'housing classes' described earlier.

1. New state-built apartments. These have been built to high standards, at high cost. They are allocated to tenants without capital payments, at very low rents. They therefore convey the largest state subsidies. To this class belong also the best of the pre-war apartments, built in the 1930s, nationalized in the 1950s, and available on the same privileged terms.
2. Older flats of lower quality, often built before the First World War, and since nationalized. Most of them are in single-storey multi-flat buildings; some are in taller buildings with balcony access from internal courtyards, or from the rear face of the building. They are of poor quality (for example two rooms, a kitchen, and no facilities), and very little money (often less than the amount of the rent) is spent on their maintenance. So, although they are available from the state on the same terms as Class I housing, their value is much less and the subsidy to their tenants is not great.
3. The best houses in the market sector, and in Hungary: villas with private gardens, and owner-occupied apartments in some bank-financed or 'condominium' apartment buildings.
4. The best of the recently-built, privately-owned, family houses. In value, these tend to fall between the better and the worse state-owned housing; they fall short of the best state-owned apartments in respect of facilities and communal services.
5. The obsolete family houses. In the cities which we researched, these houses are mostly of a fairly primitive village

character.

The three classes in the market sector enjoy varying amounts of state subsidy. The most favoured are modern apartment buildings built by the state or by co-operatives with savings bank finance, with the apartments then sold to individual owner-occupiers. These enjoy the most favourable credit facilities. They also have an effective monopoly of the available land in some of the best areas, well provided with communal services and institutions, because these areas are zoned to prohibit the building of family houses. Thus the builders of privately-owned bank-financed housing are protected from any competition by builders of family houses, and may be said to receive a land-price subsidy by favour of the state.

This tendency has developed further in other socialist countries than in Hungary. The building of family houses was stopped almost completely in the major cities of Czechoslovakia and Poland. In Prague, for example, there has been one year since the socialist transformation when as few as twenty-five family houses were built. In Poland, the volume of newly built urban family houses is insignificant, although there has been some improvement since 1971. In 1969, some 146,000 urban housing units were built in Poland of which only 14,000 were family houses; in major cities the proportion of family houses in the total is even smaller.

One consequence of the hostile attitude towards family houses is that they are forced outside the administrative boundaries of the cities. Family house building flourishes on the outskirts of Warsaw and other big Polish cities, despite high building land prices inflated by the prohibitions within the cities' boundaries. F. Gliszczynski, a noted researcher in urban agglomeration, writes:

We can observe a faster population increase outside the urban administrative boundaries, than in Warsaw itself. This, of course, does not mean the spread of the city beyond its boundaries. It is a direct result of regulations prohibiting migration to Warsaw. Besides the prohibitive effect of compulsory police registration in Warsaw, the distribution system of state-built apartments and the difficulties involved in family house building also deter people from moving to Warsaw. (1967, p. 172; see also Rocznik Statystyczny, 1970, p. 383.)

On a smaller scale, the same occurs at the outskirts of Budapest. Meanwhile, inside the city boundaries, the benefits of the policies go especially to the occupants of the privately-owned bank-financed apartments. Though these apartments are built on the most valuable land of the cities, the state charges the builders fictitious land prices which are derived from the building costs, and pay no regard at all to the value of the urban location. By contrast with these privileged land deals, the builders of family houses have to buy their land on the open market, often at high prices. The only state subsidies available to family housing are conveyed in some favourable pricing of building materials, and comparatively low rates of interest on building loans.

There remains a sixth class of housing which does not belong exclusively either to the state or to the market sector. It is the class of people without any housing of their own. These are people living with parents, in rented rooms and other sub-tenancies, or in institutional places such as workers' or students' hostels. Approximately 10 per cent of urban families belong to this class. It will be particularly interesting to find out what their chances are of moving to higher housing classes.

This is, therefore, the 'housing class structure' of Hungary's national housing system, as shown in Table 2.2.

TABLE 2.2
The national housing system in Hungary

State sector	Market sector
1. Tenants of new state-owned apartments, enjoying the highest state subsidy.	3. Owner-occupiers of bank-financed and co-operative apartments, enjoying significant subsidy.
2. Tenants of old state-owned flats, with comparatively little subsidy.	4. Builders of new family houses, with little subsidy.
	5. Owners of old family houses.
6. People without houses or flats.	

We can now proceed to examine the social contents of the various housing classes, what movement occurs between the classes and the sectors, which groups of people move from class to class, and what it costs them to move from one housing class to another.

It should first be noted that one category was omitted al-

together from the earlier description of housing classes. This is
the group of private rental flats and houses, in which tenants
rent from private landlords who for one reason or another are
not nationalized. Of the families interviewed in the Pecs–
Szeged survey 16.6 per cent were in this category. They were
then omitted from the scheme of classification, rightly or
wrongly, because they did not fit its categories: their housing
includes all three qualitative types. Also they are a dwindling
number because many of their landlords are reclaiming the
housing for themselves or their families, or selling it to their
tenants.

For English-language readers it may also be convenient to
explain that the occupation 'intellectual' stands for the wide
range of tertiary-educated people who might appear in equivalent Anglo-American classifications as 'salaried, professional,
and scientific'.

With these preliminaries, what is the relation between social
and occupational status and housing class? In the sample
survey of Pecs and Szeged, the classes of housing were occupied
as shown in Table 2.3.

Comparing the ownership with the tenants' occupations,
three tendencies are apparent:

1. Half of the high bureaucrats and salaried intellectuals live in
   apartments owned by the state and maintained by the Real
   Estate Servicing Enterprise. The proportion is still quite
   high for clerical workers, then declines as occupational
   status declines.
2. The same holds for co-operative and owner-occupied apartments: above 15 per cent of high bureaucrats and salaried
   intellectuals have them, then the proportion descends
   steeply to 1.8 per cent of unskilled workers.
3. Inverse relations hold for owner-occupied family houses:
   they house about half the unskilled workers, about a third of
   the skilled workers and technicians, and scarcely a sixth of
   the bureaucrats and intellectuals.

Other researchers in Hungary (whose works I was able to
consult in typescript) have supported the finding that family
houses are mostly built by those with lower incomes. Agnes
Losonczy found it to be true in the rural Békés county of
Hungary, in studies which are particularly valuable because all
previous surveys were of urban housing systems. I. Kemeny's

TABLE 2.3
Who owned and who occupied the housing in Pecs and Szeged in 1968?

Occupational status	Number in sample	% with first-class state housing	% with other state housing	% with own bank-financed or co-op apartment	% with own family house	% with owned housing by other private person
High bureaucrats	90	47.8	10.0	15.5	17.8	8.9
Intellectuals	128	50.0	10.9	16.4	13.3	9.4
Technicians	254	37.4	9.1	11.4	31.9	10.2
Clerical workers	112	46.4	4.5	6.2	28.6	14.3
Service workers	73	38.4	6.8	5.5	27.4	21.9
Skilled workers	473	25.3	11.6	8.0	28.2	16.9
Semi-skilled workers	271	24.4	12.2	3.7	39.9	19.8
Unskilled workers	217	23.0	10.3	1.8	48.8	16.1
Agricultural workers	36	2.8	2.8	0.0	88.9	5.5
Retired intellectuals	100	46.0	5.0	6.0	26.0	17.0
Retired workers	387	22.0	6.6	2.1	46.3	23.0

* Unless otherwise stated, data in all the following tables are from the survey conducted by the author in 1968 in two Hungarian cities Pecs and Szeged. 'Number in sample' column contains the numbers actually analysed in each table; it does not contain 'missing cases', 'no answers', etc.

research at the Csepel Iron and Metallurgical Works proved that workers, especially those poorly qualified and with low incomes, could obtain housing chiefly by building their own. Similar results were found in several districts of Budapest by the research series BUVATI conducted under the direction of Dr I. Szücs.

Figures from Czechoslovakia have shown similar tendencies. Using the 1967 nationally representative census, Jiri Vecernik (1971) related social status to the ownership of family houses. He used an index representing a composite of occupation, educational level, and income, and divided into seven grades, with grade 1 indicating the highest social status and grade 7 the lowest. The percentages of those social strata who owned family houses are shown in Table 2.4.

Generally, more of the higher social strata are to be found in the state housing sector, and more of the lower social strata in

TABLE 2.4

*Social status and owner-occupation of family houses in
Czechoslovakia in 1967*

Region	Family houses as % if all housing units	Owners of family houses as % of each social grade						
		1	2	3	4	5	6	7
Prague	29.0	26.7	31.2	18.8	29.8	25.3	41.9	38.3
Czech lands	53.4	33.5	38.4	37.9	49.3	54.3	54.4	72.5
Slovakia	77.9	36.9	61.6	64.7	58.1	78.2	86.0	87.7

(Source: J. Vecernik, 1971, p. 19)

the market sector. The picture can be further refined by comparing occupational status with type of housing tenure. In the
Hungarian sample the result was as shown in Table 2.5.

Among those with no homes of their own (who include
sub-tenants, lodgers, etc.) are 6.7 per cent of high bureaucrats
and twice that percentage of the least skilled workers. Those
with lowest status also have the highest percentage of home
owners. Those relations are reversed for tenancy, with nearly 60
per cent of the highest strata renting their housing, and only 35
per cent of the unskilled doing so.

Occupational status can also be compared with types of
building. The larger multi-storey apartment buildings tend to
be the most modern and best-equipped; with some exceptions

TABLE 2.5

Types of housing tenure according to occupational status of family head

Occupational status	Number in sample	% of tenants	% of owners	% with no housing of their own
High bureaucrats	90	58.9	34.4	6.7
Intellectuals	128	59.4	31.2	9.4
Technicians	254	46.9	44.5	8.6
Clerical workers	112	53.7	34.6	11.7
Service workers	73	50.6	34.4	15.0
Skilled workers	474	40.1	48.7	11.2
Semi-skilled workers	271	40.6	46.8	12.6
Unskilled workers	217	35.8	52.1	12.1
Agricultural workers	36	8.4	91.8	0.0
Retired intellectuals	99	58.5	32.3	9.2
Retired workers	387	44.7	48.6	6.7

noted below, smaller multi-storey buildings are usually older; flats in one-storey multi-unit buildings are oldest, poorest, and worst-equipped. Family houses range from fine villas to dirt-floored village hovels, but a high proportion have had to be built with local labour and materials, within the limited resources of their owner-occupiers. The Hungarian sample was housed as shown in Table 2.6.

TABLE 2.6
Distribution of housing according to occupational status of family head

Occupational status	Number in sample	% in larger multi-storey building with more than 10 apartments	% in smaller multi-storey building with less than 10 apartments	% in multi-unit one-storey houses	% in single-unit, one-storey houses
High bureaucrats	90	58.9	22.2	7.8	11.1
Intellectuals	125	54.4	18.4	18.4	8.8
Technicians	251	41.8	10.4	19.9	27.9
Clerical workers	111	34.2	14.5	27.0	24.3
Service workers	73	23.3	16.4	27.4	32.9
Skilled workers	470	23.4	10.9	26.6	39.1
Semi-skilled workers	268	18.3	6.7	31.3	43.7
Unskilled workers	215	12.1	12.1	29.3	46.5
Agricultural workers	35	8.6	2.9	17.1	71.4
Independent	37	18.9	8.1	21.6	51.4
Retired intellectuals	99	36.4	26.2	20.2	17.2
Retired workers	381	10.3	12.3	34.6	42.8
No occupation	117	12.8	12.8	35.1	39.3

It is again clear that families with low incomes are mostly found in family houses or in one-storey houses divided into multi-units. The latter include a good deal of the oldest and poorest housing in the state sector. Most of the best housing in both sectors goes to those with higher status.

The tables so far have not allowed much social analysis of those who live in the smaller multi-storey buildings. In Table 2.6 the aggregated data from Pecs and Szeged show comparatively little differentiation—about 20 per cent of the highest strata live in such buildings, but so also do about 12 per cent of the unskilled. But it is instructive to separate the data from Pecs alone, because in the decades before the survey an unusual number of multi-flat, multi-storey condominiums (with modern apartments for owner-occupation) had been built at

Pecs. So the proportion of new, good-quality housing was unusually high within the general category of smaller multi-storey buildings. The social occupation of the category is differentiated accordingly: 19.0 per cent of high bureaucrats and 19.4 per cent of intellectuals live in such buildings, while only 4.5 per cent of semi-skilled and 5.8 per cent of unskilled workers do so.

The relations between high status and good housing are not peculiar to Hungary. Research in other socialist countries show similar results. It is inherent in the housing economy of the East European countries that people with higher qualifications and incomes will systematically obtain large shares of the housing in new state-owned apartment buildings. W. Wesolowski and his associates (Slomczynski and Wesolowski, 1970) carried out research in three Polish cities to find the percentage of each occupational class among the occupants of new apartment buildings, and the distribution of the apartments to income classes (Tables 2.7 and 2.8).

TABLE 2.7

*Occupational status of residents in new apartment buildings
in selected cities in Poland (mid-1960s)*

Occupational status	%
Intellectuals	40.6
Technicians	22.8
Clerical workers	22.8
Service workers	15.7
Leading workers	17.4
Skilled workers	12.6
Semi-skilled and unskilled workers	8.8

TABLE 2.8

*Distribution of the apartments to income classes in selected cities
in Poland (mid-1960s)*

% of the apartments	Monthly income of the tenants (zloty)
37.3	above 4,000
34.4	3,001–4,000
18.2	2,001–3,000
10.6	below 2,000

(Source: K. Slomczynski-Wesolowski, 1970, pp. 108, 111.)

In Czechoslovakia, L. Macková (1970) observed the same high proportion of tenants with high qualifications in her examination of two preferred types of housing, the TO-6B and TO-8B apartment houses. Her findings were from 1967 data and were representative of Czech cities (Table 2.9). That

TABLE 2.9

Distribution of TO-6B and TO-8B new apartments according to occupation of family head in Bohemia in 1967

Occupational status	%
Unskilled service workers	8.2
Unskilled industrial workers	0.6
Skilled workers	32.7
Clerical workers	6.5
High bureaucrats	29.4
Intellectuals	21.0
Pensioners	1.6

(Sample of 510. Source: L. Macková, 1970, p. 10.)

picture was confirmed in L. Macková's later study (1971) of 930 tenants of new state-owned apartment buildings, from data representative of Czechoslovakia for 1970 (Table 2.10). As before—and as in Hungary—more than half of the tenants of state-owned apartment buildings are high bureaucrats or salaried intellectuals.

TABLE 2.10

Distribution of new state-owned apartments according to occupation of family head in Czechoslovakia in 1970

Occupational status	%
Workers	35.7
Intellectuals	39.7
High bureaucrats	11.6
Pensioners	6.5
Families without male head	6.4

Returning to Hungary, we may turn from the statistics to the dynamics of the system by asking how the different social strata obtained their housing (Table 2.11). Disregarding families who inherited their housing, or obtained it before adminstrative distribution began, we are left with three basic types: those who bought or built their housing, those who were given it by the state, and those who got it by exchanging other housing with or without an exchange fee.

TABLE 2.11
How families acquired their housing

Occupational status	Number in sample	% with per capita income above 1200 forints	% who built or bought housing	% awarded state housing	% through exchange	% from before 1950 or by other means
High bureaucrats	89	70.8	25.8	37.1	19.1	18.0
Intellectuals	126	63.5	20.6	39.7	18.3	21.5
Technicians	252	46.8	33.3	28.2	15.5	23.0
Clerical workers	108	40.1	25.0	26.9	20.4	27.7
Service workers	72	30.1	29.2	20.9	23.6	26.4
Skilled workers	466	32.5	34.7	24.5	11.8	29.0
Semi-skilled workers	270	23.2	35.2	24.1	13.3	27.4
Unskilled workers	217	18.0	44.2	20.8	10.1	24.9
Agricultural workers	36	8.6	55.5	8.4	2.8	32.3
Independent	37	16.7	35.2	10.8	13.5	40.5
Retired intellectuals	98	30.3	19.3	31.7	18.4	30.6
Retired workers	381	9.6	30.7	17.9	18.4	33.0

It is in the first two categories that there are noticeable social differences. Among those who built or bought their housing by their own efforts are found a modest 20.6 per cent of intellectuals and 25.8 per cent of high bureaucrats. Clerical workers also show only 25.0 per cent. With lower income groups the proportion rises fairly steeply, to 44.2 per cent of unskilled workers.

Those tendencies are reversed for the tenants of state-allocated apartments. Unskilled workers had the least chance of getting such free accommodation—only 20.8 per cent of them managed it. Meanwhile 39.7 per cent of salaried intellectuals managed it, with the high bureaucrats not far behind them.

Among those who had exchanged housing, occupation was not important. Only 10 per cent of unskilled workers had done it, but the table shows about 20 per cent of most occupations, blue-collar as well as white-collar. It should, however, be remembered that the exchanges were of diverse character.

Some were market exchanges, some were state housing exchanges. Some represented movement from the lower to the higher class of state housing, or movement into state housing. But many were exchanges within the same housing class, and were not likely to vary with occupation.

The record of how people got their housing mirrors the system's static structure, but begins also to reveal its dynamic processes. To learn more about its social dynamic, we may next ask what people had paid for their housing. If we omit those who got free housing from the state, and ask what their housing had cost those who built or bought or exchanged their houses, we should expect those in higher social strata, with generally better housing, to have paid more for it. But the expectation proves to be wrong: the findings contradict it (Table 2.12).

TABLE 2.12

Costs paid out before moving into built, bought, or exchanged housing according to occupation of family head

Occupational status	Number in sample	% paying under 20,000 forints	% paying 20–50,000 forints	% paying 50–100,000 forints	% paying over 100,000 forints
High bureaucrats	24	62.5	8.4	12.5	16.6
Intellectuals	29	55.2	27.6	3.4	13.8
Technicians	88	33.0	13.6	20.5	32.9
Clerical workers	29	24.1	13.8	17.4	44.7
Service workers	22	31.8	18.2	31.8	18.2
Skilled workers	154	24.0	14.3	24.6	37.1
Semi-skilled workers	98	19.4	11.3	38.8	30.5
Unskilled workers	83	15.7	22.9	33.7	27.7
Agricultural workers	17	11.8	41.2	29.4	17.6
Independent	12	25.0	16.7	25.0	33.3
Retired Intellectuals	19	42.1	21.1	26.3	10.5
Retired workers	103	29.1	18.4	28.2	24.3
No occupation	28	32.2	28.6	21.4	17.8

Among those who paid anything at all for their houses—which the richer groups were less likely to do—the higher occupational and income groups systematically paid less, while generally getting better housing. Thus only 37.5 per cent of the high bureaucrats and 44.8 per cent of the salaried intellectuals paid more than 20,000 forints, while about 80 per cent or more of the workers paid more than that.

In this particular analysis we were not satisfied to show only the status of the family head. We devised a complex indicator including both parents of the family, their occupations and educational levels, and the income per head of consumers in the household. The families were then distributed into five groups: high, high-middle, middle, low-middle, and low. Comparing those categories with the amounts of money paid out to buy, build, or exchange homes, the earlier findings are confirmed. Families in the high social group had averaged payments of 51,000 forints; in the high-middle group 47,000 forints; in the middle group 69,000 forints; in the low-middle group 82,000 forints; and in the low group 73,000 forints. *People in highly paid, highly qualified groups paid 22,000 forints less for their apartments—if they paid at all—than did people in poorly paid, poorly qualified, poorly placed groups.*

If people are not asked what they actually paid for their housing, but are asked what they would be willing to pay for the kind of housing they want, the same differentiation appears (Table 2.13). Among those still earning, the high bureaucrats are least prepared to pay more than 20,000 forints, and technicians and skilled workers are most willing. Families in most of

TABLE 2.13
Willingness to pay for adequate housing according to occupation of family head

Occupational status	Number in sample	Monthly income per member of family (forints)	% who would pay less than 20,000 forints	% who would pay more than 20,000 forints
High bureaucrats	12	1,627	66.7	33.3
Intellectuals	20	1,511	60.0	40.0
Technicians	39	1,244	41.0	59.0
Clerical workers	19	1,136	73.7	26.3
Service workers	15	995	66.7	33.3
Skilled workers	105	1,094	45.7	54.3
Semi-skilled workers	41	965	46.3	53.7
Unskilled workers	29	867	55.1	44.9
Retired intellectuals	14	952	71.4	28.6
Retired workers	33	789	69.7	30.3

the categories seem to have realistic views of their chances in the general competition for housing.

The discrepancies are much less if people are asked what monthly rents or mortgage instalments they would be prepared to pay. There is then not much difference between the high, high-middle and middle groups. People in the lower-middle groups would pay 290 forints for an apartment; the high group would pay 6 forints more and the high-middle group 28 forints more. This similar willingness to pay is not proportional to income, and not at all proportional to the quality of housing which the respective classes expect for their money: the higher groups want to spend a lower proportion of income to get more and better housing. (We shall return later to the detailed nature of demands.)

The willingness of the poorer groups to make greater sacrifices to get comparatively poor housing is conditioned by a history of rising prices for the poorer kinds of housing. More than half of the Hungarian housing stock deserves to be called sub-standard, but demand for it has been increasing. Two features of housing policy appear to be the main cause of this. State supplies of new urban housing have not kept up with demand; and with trifling exceptions they have all been supplied to the 'top' of the market, i.e. housing of high quality has been supplied disproportionately to people in high occupational groups. There is never quite enough even for those privileged groups; so as a general rule all new housing is pre-empted by the upper classes and no new housing (except what they build arduously for themselves) is available to the lower classes. Substantial proportions of people in those lower occupational groups therefore have to compete with each other for the older and poorer housing stock. That stock is steadily reduced by condemnations and demolitions. The numbers competing for it increase with the growth of urban population. Besides that simple market pressure there is some additional, 'artificial' pressure. To be possessed of some sort of housing, however poor, can be a first step—but a difficult one—towards bargaining for advantages in the state housing sector, especially in the black market exchanges which occur in some local government sectors of state housing. So those who want poor private housing to live in sometimes have to compete not only against each other, but against other interests as well.

This understanding of the processes had been supported by our earlier studies—there were scarcely any unskilled workers in the new multi-storey estates. The survey of Pecs and Szeged confirms the same picture. Increasing demand for diminishing supplies of poorer housing has the effect of increasing its price, both in the bilateral sales between private owners which are lawfully made at market prices, and in the illegal 'fees' or 'down payments' which are often paid for the acquisition or exchange of housing in the local authority sector. If the resultant prices are not actually inverse to the quality of the housing, they certainly do not reflect the real housing costs or values. In the early 1970s, for example, it was common for full-sized apartments with all facilities to be priced only twice as high as single rooms: people were paying 84,000 forints for apartments with full facilities, 58,000 forints for apartments with half facilities, 53,000 forints for a room and kitchen with no facilities, and 44,000 forints for single rooms. The pattern of rents show similar distortions: only a quarter of the high bureaucrats and intellectuals who pay rent pay more than 200 forints a month, while a similar proportion of unskilled workers pay similar rents for much poorer accommodation.

We can now roughly characterize the movements of the different social classes in and between the housing classes detailed in our analysis.

In the lowest class of state housing, consisting of obsolete state-owned housing administered by local authorities, we find increasing proportions of blue-collar workers. Intellectuals also start their housing progress in this sector, but most of them soon move on. Some of them 'exchange up' to the best state housing; others buy into the co-operative or strata-title apartments which can be bought from state builders. There many stay permanently, but some move over to the best of the garden villas available in the market sector. In the top class of state apartments there is a range of occupations from skilled workers to high bureaucrats; from among that population is is usually only the intellectuals and high bureaucrats who move on to co-operative apartments or garden villas. To do so, they have access to the best available housing credit; they borrow and buy on distinctly better terms than do most ordinary families who buy or build ordinary family houses.

Next after the villas and private apartments, the second

market class consists of the better family houses. This category is doubly important because it includes the dominant type of new housing construction in the larger provincial towns, and because it is the main housing resource of the more successful strata of blue-collar workers. Good new family houses tend to be occupied by technicians of modest means, some skilled workers, and many of the more successful of the semi-skilled and un-skilled. To get this sort of housing in the cities is easier for families who already have housing of some sort to sell or exchange. Those who do not have such resources, and who have not been able to inherit or save deposits, are left to occupy the lowest classes of housing in both sectors. The obsolete local-authority housing has already been mentioned. The third and lowest category in the market sector is physically similar, or worse. Its population is comparatively stable: many families are trapped or stranded in this old slum housing, waiting or hoping or saving to move out of it one day, and meanwhile perhaps doing the minor improvements which are all that the local authorities permit in the older areas. This is the housing to which most of the homeless come. It is also used, usually for shorter periods, by some of the more skilled workers' families, especially by young or migrating households.

In a very rough and approximate way, the predominant pattern of housing mobility may be represented graphically. In Figure 2.1, illustrating housing mobility, the people are divided for simplicity into two income classes only, a 'higher' and a 'lower'.

In summary, with all due allowances for individual varia-tions, the trends are as follows: the social groups with higher incomes move steadily towards the highest housing classes in the state and market sectors, and come close to monopolizing them. Below that, the highest class of housing available to most of those with lower incomes is the second market class, i.e. the range of family houses omitting the superior 'villa' category. The housing options and opportunities of these lower classes are limited more by the state policies which allocate state housing and credit than by the people's capacities to pay. Public policy thus provides that, on average, the richer classes get better housing for less money and effort, while the poorer classes get worse housing at the cost of more money or effort, or both.

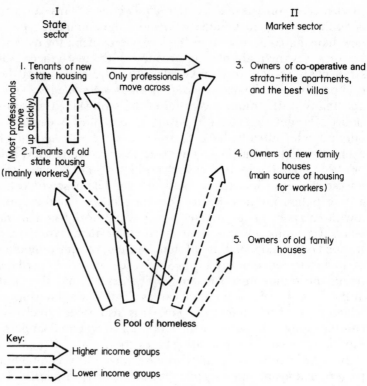

FIG 2.1   Housing mobility

Housing mobility and social status

In trying to follow the housing progress of different social groups over time, we encountered some methodological problems. The households surveyed in Pecs and Szeged were asked for information about their previous housing and their housing movements—but only if they had moved house since 1950. The data derived from these questions do not cover families whose existing housing was their first in the city, or their first ever if the household was first formed after 1950 in the house it still occupied in 1968. In all 1500 families—two-thirds of the 2,300 surveyed—gave information about their earliest housing situation, and the remaining third did not. That missed third may distort some of the conclusions drawn from the survey. The 33 per cent omitted from the sample include families newly formed since 1950, and families who immigrated into the city since that date. In the summaries neither group figures as having improved their housing situation, though some may well have done so if individuals moved from worse accommodation in other households to form new households in better accommodation. (Any reverse effects would likewise be omitted from the data.) Those excluded from the survey may also include some of another group, that of socially and geographically static elderly families, especially owners of family houses who belong in the middle categories of occupation and housing class in our scheme of analysis. We cannot assess the combined effect of these various omissions; but some of them would affect the results in opposite ways, and, while there is of course no ground for supposing that they cancel one another exactly, we believe that they would be unlikely to reverse, or even substantially modify, the tendencies apparent in the 67 per cent sample. We do, therefore, tabulate the data from the 67 per cent and treat them as if true for 100 per cent; we concede that the grounds for doing so are imperfect, but note that the results accord well with the better-based results detailed in the previous section.

If we categorize the housing by number of rooms, density of people per room, number of facilities, etc., and categorize the families by the occupations of their heads, then ask how the occupational groups held or changed their housing categories over time, we can observe three trends: (1) there was a general improvement of the housing situation of all social strata; (2) some social groups improved their housing faster than others, with the effect of increasing the housing differentials between social strata; (3) there was increasing correlation between social status and housing class.

The general improvement in the housing situation is most obvious in the falling numbers of homeless and of households living as boarders. Sixty-eight per cent of the responding families had been tenants, service occupiers, or owners of their previous housing; 90 per cent had those tenures now. A main motive for moving house was evidently a desire for more room. Sixty-six per cent had previously lived in flats of one room and kitchen; only 49 per cent did so now. Those movements had lowered the living densities: the proportion living at more than two persons per room had fallen from 53 to 24 per cent. There were also improvements in quality and facilities. Twenty-five per cent had a bathroom in their previous housing, 51 per cent had one now. Twenty-five per cent had piped water previously, 65 per cent had it now. Asked for their own judgements, 65 per cent of the families thought their present housing better than their previous housing, 13 per cent did not notice any difference, and 22 per cent perceived a change for the worse. Whatever bias the detailed figures may conceal, there was undoubtedly some net improvement of the housing situation as a whole. Construction since 1950 had improved the stock, quickened the ordinary rhythms of filtering and housing mobility. Thirty per cent of the families had moved into their present homes between 1951 and 1960, and 42 per cent between 1961 and 1968. Mobility may not have accelerated as much as those figures suggest, because some of the 'mobiles' of the 1950s may have died or emigrated before the survey. But the overall rate of mobility is quite high, and also general: no social group in either of the two cities failed to improve its housing situation.

That general improvement was not however due entirely, or mainly, to state construction or state distribution. Since 1950 only 14.7 per cent of families had obtained housing from local authorities and only 9.5 per cent had service housing. State provisions thus accounted for less than 25 per cent, and the proportion was still under 30 per cent if stretched to include state housing acquired by exchange. It was left to more than two-thirds to acquire housing in some other way: 15 per cent built, 18 per cent bought, more than 10 per cent made private exchanges, 20 per cent inherited, 7.7 per cent were in houses of which they had been tenants before 1950. Thus individual effort, hard-working self-help and mutual help, and family connections and inheritance provided for many more families than did the state's much-publicized housing activities.

At the risk of getting ahead of ourselves we may press that comparison further, to ask whether different policies might have achieved rather more improvement through those decades, as well as distributing it better. If state resources had not been concentrated on supplying free or near-free housing to the privileged minority, but had instead been distributed more widely in the form of credits and subsidies to augment the private resources of individual buyers and builders, then the same public resources might have served to mobilize rather larger resources of individual savings and initiative. And if the state had not limited private construction and reconstruction in older areas by its credit policies, its planning policies in some areas, and its rigid concentration and monopoly of all substantial building construction, then the resources of householders and independent tradesmen might have produced more new houses, and also more and better reconstruction or replacement of older housing in the neglected older areas of the cities. Though impossible to prove, we believe such alternative policies might have done a good deal to improve the general housing situation. They might well also have gone beyond improvements to move the society closer to its general social and political goals by reducing housing inequalities between income classes, instead of increasing them.

We return to the analysis to compare the success of the different occupational strata, over time, in moving from smaller to larger accommodation (Table 2.14). Similar differences appear in the density of occupation, i.e. the space per head that

TABLE 2.14
How occupational groups got bigger houses

Occupational status	% whose *previous* home had 2 rooms or more		% whose *present* home has 2 rooms or more		% who improved
High bureaucrats	58.9		79.6		20.7
Intellectuals	46.9		75.5		28.6
Technicians	39.6		66.6		27.0
Clerical workers	42.1	Range of	55.8	Range of	13.7
Service workers	32.7	inequality	42.8	inequality	10.1
Skilled workers	26.1	31.8	50.1	50.1	24.0
Semi-skilled workers	25.5		37.0		11.5
Unskilled workers	27.1		29.5		2.4

families have (Table 2.15; the official norm was two persons per room throughout those decades). We can now repeat the exercise for piped water (Table 2.16) and for bathrooms (Table 2.17).

Together the four tables 2.14, 2.15, 2.16, and 2.17 prove that: (1) all social groups improved their housing: (2) in all items the

TABLE 2.15
How occupational groups got more room per head

Occupational status	% under 2 per room in *previous* home		% under 2 per room in *present* home		% who improved
High bureaucrats	64.2		93.3		29.1
Intellectuals	62.5		90.5		28.0
Technicians	47.4		79.6		32.2
Clerical workers	57.9	Range of	78.0	Range of	20.1
Service workers	48.0	inequality	69.9	inequality	21.9
Skilled workers	40.5	28.6	67.5	36.8	27.0
Semi-skilled workers	34.1		59.5		25.4
Unskilled workers	35.6		56.5		20.9

range of inequality between the highest and lowest groups increased; and (3) the groups which made the greatest progress were some middle and upper-middle groups: technicians, intellectuals, and skilled workers.

If we add the percentages who improved from all four tables, the totals offer a crude sort of index of the housing improvement achieved by each group. They are shown in Table 2.18.

In summary, the gap between the top and bottom widened, but there was at the same time some degree of levelling within the upper ranks, as the greatest 'filtering' progress was achieved by some middle and upper-middle groups. It is noticeable that

TABLE 2.16
How occupational groups got piped water

Occupational status	% who had piped water in *previous* home		% who have piped water in *present* home		% who improved
High bureaucrats	55.2		95.6		40.6
Intellectuals	52.6		96.8		44.2
Technicians	35.8		83.5		47.7
Clerical workers	31.4	Range of	83.9	Range of	52.5
Service workers	30.0	inequality	68.5	inequality	38.5
Skilled workers	20.4	36.7	67.5	47.6	47.1
Semi-skilled workers	22.0		56.5		34.4
Unskilled workers	18.5		48.0		29.5

TABLE 2.17
How occupational groups got bathrooms

Occupational status	% with bathroom in *previous* home		% with bathroom in *present* home		% who improved
High bureaucrats	60.3		88.9		28.6
Intellectuals	62.1		88.1		26.0
Technicians	38.6		74.5		35.9
Clerical workers	35.1	Range of inequality 52.5	69.4	Range of inequality 59.7	34.3
Service workers	21.2		46.6		25.4
Skilled workers	18.8		56.7		37.9
Semi-skilled workers	11.8		36.9		25.1
Unskilled workers	7.8		29.2		21.4

those most successful groups were of people who had to achieve their status at least partly by skill and education, and not solely by political or administrative appointment. Their talents or training may have had some effect on their housing preferences, and the value they put on the quality of their housing.

To explain the double significance of differentiation and levelling, we next show how far the housing situation of each group deviates from the overall average. For example, the proportion of families with apartments of two rooms or more was 33.9 per cent previously, and 46.5 at the time our survey was carried out. If we designate those proportions as zero, we can then indicate with positive or negative values how far each occupational group deviates above or below that norm. Table 2.19 does that for two important indicators of housing situation,

TABLE 2.18
Occupational groups in order of housing improvements achieved

Occupational status	%
Technicians	142.8
Skilled workers	136.0
Intellectuals	126.8
Clerical workers	120.6
High bureaucrats	119.0
Semi-skilled workers	96.4
Service workers	95.9
Unskilled workers	74.2

TABLE 2.19
Occupational groups' changing deviation from housing norms

Occupational status	% who had 2 rooms or more	% who have 2 rooms or more	% who had bathroom	% who have bathroom
High bureaucrats	+25.0	+32.9	+34.8	+37.5
Intellectuals	+13.0	+28.8	+36.6	+36.7
Technicians	+5.7	+20.1	+13.1	+23.1
Clerical workers	+8.2	+9.3	+9.6	+18.0
Service workers	−1.2	−13.4	−4.3	−4.8
Skilled workers	−7.8	+3.6	−6.7	+5.3
Semi-skilled workers	−8.4	−9.5	−13.7	−14.5
Unskilled workers	−6.8	−17.0	−17.7	−22.2

the proportions of each occupational group who have two rooms or more, and the proportions who have bathrooms.

As a final measure we can list a number of the housing items in 'order of inequality'. This is arrived at by observing the difference between the percentage of the highest group who enjoy the norm or facility, and the percentage of the lowest group who do so. The largest difference is for bathrooms, 59.7. Then follow size of apartment 50.1, piped water 46.6, and density of people per room, 36.8.

The next step is to compare the actual situation and progress of the occupational groups with their subjective perceptions and expectations. In actual situation, the high bureaucrats had the best housing arrangements in the past, and have the best still. There are signs that their housing demands begin to be saturated: starting from the higher level their deviation from the average has diminished, and their rate of improvement has slowed compared with that of some other groups. The intellectuals have made faster progress, and even outstripped the class above them absolutely in one or two respects. Together those two top groups make up about 10 per cent of the population. The technicians have improved their housing fastest of all. Starting worse off than the clerical workers, they are now rapidly approaching the housing standards and aspirations of the highest groups. The clerical workers' progress has been sluggish: technicians and skilled workers have overtaken them in income, and correspondingly in housing. (Technicians, clerical workers, and retired intellectuals together make up about 20 per cent of the population.) Service workers have improved their housing very moderately, falling further behind the national average in a number of respects. Semi-skilled workers have done marginally better than service workers, but poorly compared with most groups and national averages. (Skilled, semi-skilled, and service workers make up about 25 per cent of the population.) Unskilled workers have made the least progress: they gained a little on the national average in plumbing facilities, but fell further behind in some other items including the size of their housing. Together with other groups who have similar housing and a similar incapacity to improve it much— agricultural workers, retired blue-collar workers, unemployed, and other pensioners—they make up the remainder, which is nearly half, of the urban society.

Before proceeding further it is as well to notice one feature of these comparisons between occupational groups which might otherwise mislead the unwary. The picture of different occupational groups improving their housing situations at varying rates—e.g. technicians improving their housing faster than clerical workers—is in one respect misleading. Some of the groups, including the high bureaucrats, the clerical workers, and the unskilled, have comparatively stable numbers and composition over the decades. So it is indeed high bureaucrats or clerical workers who have poorer housing at the beginning of the period and better housing at the end of it. But it is otherwise with groups whose numbers and composition changed rapidly through the period as a result of rapid industrialization and technical change. The technician who has a better house now may well have been a peasant or labourer, not a technician at all, when he had worse housing a decade ago. His group has increased rapidly in numbers and status, and his housing improvement is related to that socio-economic change. Our studies did not distinguish the housing improvement achieved by those who had been in their present occupational group throughout the period, from the housing improvement achieved by those who had changed their occupational status as well as their housing during the period.

With these cautions in mind, we may now turn to the satisfaction which the different groups expressed with their housing situation. Of the high bureaucrats, who had the best housing, 66.3 per cent loved their housing. But at the other extreme unskilled workers, having the worst housing, did not express a corresponding dissatisfaction with it. Almost half—49.8 per cent—said they were satisfied with it.

Service workers and semi-skilled workers had slightly better housing than the unskilled, but more of them were dissatisfied with it. Their rate of housing improvement remained low, but many of them were beginning to regard their housing as a symbol of status, and to perceive a contradiction between their (better) social status and their (backward) housing situation. It was predictable that they would press their housing claims hard through the coming decade, when their numbers were also likely to increase from various economic causes. But the two groups would not press *the same* claims: in the nature of their jobs and aspirations the service workers would mostly look to the local authorities to provide them with better housing, while the semi-skilled would follow their skilled mates in working and saving for the better family houses in the market sector.

As noted above, people's satisfaction with their housing does not vary as widely as their actual housing situation does. That is illustrated in another way by comparing people in one-roomed flats with people who complain that they are short of space. Of the high bureaucrats, 27.3 per cent complain that they are short of space, though only 19.1 per cent of the group live in one-roomed flats. Among technicians the values are closer—27.2 per cent feel short of space, 29.2 per cent live in one-roomed flats. After that the curves cross on the graph: from the clerical workers on through the remaining occupational groups, more and more people live in one-roomed flats but less and less complain about it. At the extreme, 66 per cent of unskilled workers live in one-roomed flats but only 40 per cent express dissatisfaction with the number of rooms they have.

The groups are most alike in their future housing intentions. Who wants to move house? Eighty per cent of high bureaucrats intend to stay where they are, and so do 74.9 per cent of unskilled workers—the number of unskilled who intend to move is actually exceeded by the number of intellectuals who intend to move.

Putting together these various ways of measuring group differences, we can see that the difference between the highest and lowest groups' real access to housing advantages varied from 30 to 50 per cent; their expressed satisfaction with their housing showed a narrower variation of 15 or 20 per cent; their intention to move varied by a mere 5 per cent. Our conclusion from this 'narrowing' pattern of realities, feelings, and intentions is that the groups appraise their housing chances realistically, and do not invite disappointment by indulging in impractical hopes or expectations. The pattern is not evidence that the poorer groups have lower housing needs or rights: it merely shows that they are well aware of their restricted possibilities.

The same sober realism appears in people's expressed desires for specific improvements. Asked what size of house they would like to move to, 23.2 per cent of unskilled workers said they would like one-roomed flats; less than 10 per cent of other groups wanted as little space as that. Half of the high bureaucrats and intellectuals wanted three rooms or more; in all other groups, between half and two-thirds would be satisfied with two-roomed apartments. In the matter of facilities, most people wanted bathrooms—but from 15 to 20 per cent of the blue-collar groups would be content with a washing alcove.

To sum up: from 1950 to 1968 class inequalities in housing did not diminish, they increased. Moreover, the development pattern of occupational expectations and aspirations did not suggest that the current housing system would reverse the trend, or reduce housing inequalities, in the foreseeable future. But the people themselves were not generally conscious of increasing housing inequalities, or depressed by them, chiefly because the housing situation of all classes had visibly improved through the years.

The malfunctioning of the housing system

We have shown that the state distribution of housing systematically favours the higher income groups, both in housing quality and in subsidized housing costs. Lower income groups generally have to improve their poorer housing by building or buying at market prices. The small numbers from the latter groups who do not get housing from public authorities get it within a system of graded housing exchanges. For that and other reasons a similar bias tends to hold among the families of all classes to get their housing by their own efforts: the richer groups pay less for better housing, the poorer groups pay more in money or labour to get poorer housing. This latter discrimination arises partly from discriminatory credit and exchange policies, and partly from the richer groups' possession of more valuable housing inherited from the previous regime.

We have also shown that the housing system's class inequalities have been polarized and increased by state housing policies, and continue to increase despite the absolute improvement of the housing situation of all classes.

The history of public statements and policy directives meanwhile leaves no doubt that this further unequalization is not the official purpose of state housing policy. Its official purpose is to reduce housing inequalities. We conclude that the system has not been working properly, either before or after an official attempt to reform it in 1971.

Furthermore it is not only in its housing role that housing policy has been malfunctioning. The ostensible purpose of state housing activity was to see that the inequalities of income generated by incentive pay differentials in the economy as a whole should *not* be reflected in equivalent housing inequalities. It was to prevent precisely that effect, that housing was declared to be a right not a market commodity, to be taken out of the market for administrative distribution instead. But the actual administration has not only given the better housing to those with higher incomes. It has given it at less cost, with higher state subsidy, than is available to poorer income groups. So, besides increasing housing inequalities, the housing policy has also increased effective income inequalities, making the real income differences *greater* than the wage-fixing authorities presumably thought necessary for purposes of productive incentive and reward.

In exposing the mechanisms which have these anti-social effects we nevertheless emphasize that we believe they were inevitable in the circumstances. They flowed from impulses towards housing equality, and from the logic of policies of equality applied in conditions of scarcity. They cannot be written off as perversions to be blamed on avoidable bureaucratic bias or corruption.

A housing policy based on the principle of equality must, before anything else, decide how to distribute scarce housing. An obvious first response to the problem is to ordain distribution according to need. That principle did have some real effect in the early years of socialist transformation, when some luxury housing was subdivided or shared to house more and needier people than it had housed before. But for most available housing, including all new housing, it did not take long to discover that need is an inadequate criterion in a poor country where nearly everyone is needy. There were and are cities with twenty genuinely 'needy' or 'entitled' applications for every new apartment built. When need exceeds supply so overwhelmingly, it is scarcely practicable to assure impartial distribution by the next conventional device, which is queueing—'rationing by waiting time'. A waiting time of ten or fifteen or even twenty years defeats its own purpose: there is no reason at all to suppose that today's needs are accurately or impartially measured by listings done ten or twenty years ago. The distributing authorities therefore had to look for some auxiliary principle. They continued to recognize acute or desperate need—to do them justice, they have usually rehoused people whose existing housing is so physically bad as to threaten accident or illness. But, just as social need is too general a category, physical danger is too restrictive. The authorities still need some further principle to decide the bulk of each day's allocations. So— through most of Eastern Europe—they choose 'social merit', though of course its definition varies widely . If too many claimants are needy, housing should go to those who contribute most to the common good, who deserve housing as a reward, and who may perhaps also have the greatest capacity to appreciate good housing. The official directives about housing allocation enjoined some preference for productive workers. Beyond that legal requirement, the allocating authorities could exercise their own discretion in defining social merit, and rewarding it with housing and housing subsidies.

If the stock of housing is limited, and also has built-in inequalities between unit and unit, it is hard to object to a principle which allocates it in some relation to social merit and usefulness. (Any reader who doubts this should try to imagine operating any opposite principle, under which *worse* work or behaviour would be the citizen's only way to get better housing.) Nevertheless, allocation to merit has been responsible for the great paradox of the early socialist policies: society already rewarded its more useful members with higher incomes, and now its determination to *equalize* their housing situation was in practice *unequalizing* it, and further unequalizing the real incomes as well.

We repeat our view that the paradox was intrinsic in the policies; it was not a matter of bureaucratic corruption. While the same bureaucrats were redistributing both the incomes and the housing inherited from the previous regime, they were successful and effective in reducing the inequalities of the 1930s. It was when the reorganized society established its permanent new divisions of labour and rates of pay that the new social differentiation inevitably emerged—and the effect of the new income and housing policies was *to superimpose one reward pattern on another to produce a wider range of inequality than either policy originally intended.*

How should these tendencies be corrected? We know that the East European socialist society is still a stratified one, which necessarily rates and rewards its members according to their usefulness and their contribution to the common good. Because housing is so important to people, we accept that they will use some part of their differentiated incomes to differentiate their housing to some degree. We can even accept that housing differentials may have some useful social functions as 'over-award payments'; if the wage differentials do not adequately reflect the people's working differentials or incentive needs, then housing differences may function as covert 'wage supplements'. Something of that kind certainly seemed to be at work, whether justified or not, in Hungary. It was national policy to distribute new industrial growth to many centres; but it was well known that many of the new industries, prevented by national wage controls from offering wage incentives, had difficulty in attracting young technicians and skilled workers to provincial towns unless they could offer good housing—which they accordingly did.

The use of housing as a wage supplement—i.e. as an additional reward for a whole class of occupation or skill—is understandable. But it is a different matter to use housing as a *work incentive*. For that purpose it is unsuitable, and a moment's reflection should be enough to understand why. A good apartment given free is worth many years of a worker's wages, and takes many more years of repayments if he has to pay for it. In neither case is it rational to use a long-term commitment (which subsidized housing represents) as a day-by-day work incentive. Some of the industrial enterprises discovered their mistake when skilled workers attracted by good housing moved into company flats, then left the enterprise after a year or two for other jobs but remained as occupants of company housing.

Whatever the real value of housing as a work incentive, it has undoubtedly been used for that purpose in Eastern Europe. Whether there was any real need to use it thus as an additional reward, to correct the faults of a wage policy which offered insufficient differentiation in money income, is beyond the scope of this study. That is a central question of social and economic policy, and it is central to any understanding of stratification in socialist society. We cannot resolve it here; but our understanding of the housing system leads to the conclusion that the basic policies of social and economic distribution made it nearly inevitable that the new housing policies should have the unintended effects which our analysis has revealed.

The same logic has defeated most attempts so far to improve the distribution of housing by detailed reforms of its management. Through the 1960s the Hungarian press repeatedly noticed that families with above-average incomes were moving into the new apartment estates, and that new housing developments seemed to need suspiciously large car parks. There were various official attempts to democratize housing distribution: administrative procedures were reviewed, social committees were set up, the names of those who got the new housing were listed on council notice boards. But, if our analysis is true, those attempts were ineffective because they were directed at an insoluble problem.

In May 1970 the Hungarian party and government announced some new housing policies, which were implemented during 1971. As far as they went, the changes were in general accord with the conclusions of our research. The main new principle was that *rents should reflect the value of the housing*. Properly applied that would heavily increase the rents of good state-owned apartments; that and a cessation of 'free' housing allocation would certainly improve social distribution, and bring its realities into plainer view. But in practice nothing so drastic was to happen in any near future. To stop the regressive subsidies altogether would involve a revolution in rent and price structures. The statement of May 1970 accompanied its new principles with new compromises. Having declared that rents should reflect the value of housing, it proceeded to define the value of housing as the cost of maintaining it. That is about as sensible as fixing the price of shoes at the cost of cleaning them. Other new principles announced in the same statement would be slow to take effect because they concerned building policy, whose effects on the whole housing stock are necessarily slow. But beginnings are better than nothing, and (again in accord with our research) the state builders would now begin to differentiate the design of new rental apartments, so that new estates could include some modest, lower-cost apartments for tenants of modest means. There would also be some new arrangements for co-operatives, which might make it easier to build new flats for blue-collar workers.

To recapitulate: on the one hand, occupants of houses should pay economic rents, to prevent concealed benefits going to the well-off. On the other hand the more extensive the reliance on market pricing, the more necessary it may be to provide subsidized 'social housing' to some low-income groups, to avoid hardship. (Some such welfare housing is provided in all industrialized countries.)

But relations between 'market' and 'social' distribution are capable of paradox, and need to be well understood. In capitalist conditions it may be possible to distribute 'social' housing to the poorest households. But that is not possible if there is no market sector at all, so that *all* housing is 'social'. If income inequalities have been set at some socialist minimum, it is not rational or remotely practicable then to *reduce* these deliberately-chosen differentials—and upset every natural expectation of the citizens—by distributing housing benefits *inversely* to income. If there is no market and all housing is 'social', it is practically unavoidable that housing must become a positive part of the reward system, so that administrative distribution will be 'from the top down', will add further to income inequalities, and will rarely reach to the poorest at all.

In Hungary, as in most of Eastern Europe, administrative and market distribution coexist, but they coexist in proportions critically different, and in conditions critically different, from those found in capitalist countries, and the administrative distributions have tended on balance to follow the model of 'distribution from the top down' rather than 'from the bottom up'. At the same time, the socialist countries have sufficient protections to prevent the gross unequalizing effects which market distribution can have in capitalist countries. In that combination of conditions we believe that the way to better distribution of housing in the socialist countries is by careful extensions of market distribution, with some reform where necessary of the mechanisms of regulation, credit, private building, etc., to ensure that the market remains accessible to the lower earners.

In the light of those considerations, the Hungarian reform of 1971 took a step in the right direction, even if the step was a very modest one. Its principles were right, but were heavily compromised, with state distribution remaining as the central instrument of housing policy. Though we do not have later figures, the malfunctions described above have certainly continued. There is some danger that the reform may lead the responsible leaders of state and local authorities to believe they have 'solved the housing problem', and to suppose that all it needs now is a massive construction programme. In fact the reform can fulfil no such sanguine expectations unless the 1971 ordinances are perceived as merely the first step in the right direction. Without further and longer steps, those first ones may have negligible effects. As a first example of their limitations, the cautious rent increases in the summer of 1971 somewhat reduced the subsidies enjoyed by tenants of good-quality state apartments—until the building material price increases of 1 January 1972 effectively neutralized their effects and restored the tenants' comparative advantages.

We shall return later to these social and political implications of the housing economy. But we must first examine the other half of the 'vicious circle' by asking how, and to what extent, the differences between people's housing situations affect their living conditions and their families' mobility.

Social consequences of housing inequalities

Differences of housing quality, and different housing chances for different social strata, do not by themselves constitute a social problem. We argued earlier that the housing system becomes a social problem only if people become conscious that it is creating unjust inequalities. When people come to believe that they suffer from that cause, they commonly believe that their poor housing situation hinders their individual chances and their full social integration.

There is wide agreement among social researchers that social

moralities are prompted heavily by concern for the next generation. Even if we accept the use of housing as a social reward
(which we do not), and accordingly accept that people in poor
housing deserve no better, we still think it both unfair and
socially inefficient that such punishment of parents should be
allowed to damage their children's chances, including their
chances of social or housing mobility. 'Unfair' is a moral judge-
ment; but it can also be said to be inefficient for a dynamic
society, if dynamism is more widely valued than fair distribution.

The question of the dynamism or 'openness' of society is not
central to our argument, but it is worth some brief discussion
because of its implications for housing policy. If it is argued that
a society should try to offer open and equal opportunities to all
its members, in order to allow the greatest mobility of which the
population is capable, it is sometimes objected that mobility
can be 'optimal' or it can be excessive, and excess should not be
encouraged. Some parties in Hungary argue that the decline of
mobility there is natural, after the exaggerated mobility of the
years immediately following the Second World War. There is
also an economic argument to the effect that optimal economic
efficiency would exploit family differences deliberately: if an
educational system wants to produce the best skills at least cost,
it should select the most promising talents from the most
promising family backgrounds. It can produce skills more
cheaply that way than it can possibly do if it is first required to
equalize all children's opportunities by giving most attention to
those with the worst backgrounds. We cannot pursue here the
question of 'optimum mobility'. Like the question of 'functional
social inequalities' it belongs with general problems of social
stratification which are beyond the scope of this study. But we
can satisfy one requirement of scientific objectivity by making
our own values explicit on this basic question. We believe that,
if we want a dynamic society, we must reject any avoidable
blocking or limiting of mobility. But it does not follow that
removing limitations will always or necessarily increase mobility, because the members of society will still decide for themselves which possibilities to pursue, and which not. When no
material or institutional constraints remain, there may still be
cultural or ideological constraints. Constraints of either kind
are capable, moreover, of working either way, to reduce mobil-

ity or to over-encourage it. We do not think that any spontaneous, freely-chosen mobility should be regarded as excessive;
excessive mobility is possible, but only if it is forced by some
exercise of central will on people who do not want it.

Questions of mobility have long been linked with questions of
housing policy especially by sociologists. People's housing
situations affect their chances of individual mobility and social
integration. Sociologists played a large part in discovering those
relations, and in bringing the knowledge to bear on the ideology
of equal opportunity. The ideologists of capitalism were eager
to convince the world that, when capitalism had removed the
legal constraints and discriminations of feudal society, it had
thereby equalized everybody's opportunities of rising to the
top. An open road for everyman 'from log cabin to White
House'—or from errand-boy to millionaire in the private
sector—was especially celebrated in the American Dream, in
which economists have at times been prone to share. Sociologists have been less prone: decade after decade of research has
shown 'equal opportunity' to be a hollow slogan wherever there
are basic inequalities in material and social conditions. In
unequal conditions, opportunities are never equal.

In Hungary there have been some distinguished investigations of social and educational mobility. (See Ferge, 1969; Mód,
Ferge, Láng, and Kémeny, 1966; Andorka, 1970.) They make
clear that different occupational groups display different
mobility. Other investigations converge with those to suggest
the hypothesis that people in different housing classes also have
different mobility.

We observed earlier, in connection with housing mobility,
that previous sociological studies of housing did not seem to us
to have paid enough attention to the macro-sociology of
housing. Neither in Hungary nor in more advanced countries,
at the time when our studies began, had the mechanisms of
interaction between social structures and housing systems been
systematically mapped to show the detailed effects of each upon
the other. There were bits and pieces of research, chiefly into
some physical and psychological and social effects of bad
housing conditions. For example, W. C. Loring (1956) had
shown a relation between very high residential density and
some symptoms of social disorganization. In a study cited
earlier, P. H. Chombart de Lauwe (1959–60) found connections

between housing conditions and conflicts within families. R. E. Mitchell (1971) has since found a fairly weak correlation between residential density and family structure on the one hand and various indicators of social pathology on the other. It is regrettable that the results of our Hungarian survey are not suitable for methodical mapping. All they can support are some hypotheses for further investigation, and it is only in that tentative way that we now summarize some of them.

There is obviously a strong relation between housing conditions and children's progress at school. The relation is strongest of all with residential density (in the sense of people per room), and there was abundant evidence of it in the data from Pecs and Szeged. But the causal importance of the housing conditions is increasingly difficult to isolate. Children's progress is related to housing density, but it is related even more strongly to father's occupation and to parents' educational levels.

Table 2.20 shows the average school results of general school pupils at Pecs and Szeged in relation to the living density of their homes; and Table 2.21 gives the same educational indi-

TABLE 2.20
Relationship of school results to living density

Density: square metres of floor per head	Child's average school result
Less than 5	3.2
5.1 to 8	3.3
8.1 to 12	3.7
12.1 to 16	3.9
16.1 to 20	4.1
over 20	3.9

TABLE 2.21
Relationship of school results to mother's education

Mother's education	Child's average school results
Less than Grade 8	3.5
Grade 8–11	3.7
High School leaving	4.1
University or other tertiary	4.6

cator in relation to the educational level of the children's mothers. There are similar correlations with father's occupation and father's educational level. But—perhaps as a warning against simplistic interpretation—the tables still conceal some surprises. The Pecs and Szeged children perform similarly for social status and parents' educational level, but in relations between living density and school progress the cities differ significantly.

The family's social status, including parents' occupation and educational level, is related to living density. So it is not surprising that, when the figures are controlled for social status, the effect of living density on school progress is dramatically reduced. R. E. Mitchell (1971, p. 27) found that, when other factors were controlled, the social consequences of living density appeared to be slight—and his findings are especially challenging because they relate to Hong Kong where living density is extraordinarily high. Our Hungarian study yields similar results if, instead of school results, we examine parents' aspirations for their children. Our tentative hypothesis is that housing situation is an intervening variable. Its effects on social mobility vary with circumstances. They seem to be strongest where housing differences are physically distributed to produce segregation of the housing classes from each other. Bad housing has most effect when it occurs in slum areas. Our data also suggest that the social effects of housing circumstances are greatest where poor housing exists at high density, with segregation; as we move from these to normal or better housing circumstances, the traceable social effect of the housing circumstances declines and eventually disappears altogether.

It would be interesting to go beyond children's mobility to see whether housing circumstances have a more general influence on families' work or social integration. The problems of measurement are even harder, but we would expect to find that some housing circumstances have significant effects and others do not. L. Burns and associates discovered some complicated correlations when they investigated the effect of housing circumstances on productivity. (See Burns, Thompson, and Tjios, 1965.) They found that better housing improved workers' productivity up to a point, but not beyond it. The 'ceiling' may have reflected the fact that it was welfare housing, whose tenants could lose their housing entitlement if their earnings reached a certain level. We do not know of any comparable study of relations between housing and productivity in Hungary.

Besides any effects it may have on productivity or on children's chances, a family's housing situation obviously affects its social situation and possibilities in other ways. It affects the possibilities of local contact and friendship (which may sometimes affect the possibilities of mobility). It can affect consumer habits and recreational possibilities. Studies of consumer patterns indicate that they can be greatly affected when people move house. Moving from lodgings into an apartment of its own can affect a family's budget and life-style for years to come; the effects are even greater when workers spend years building their own houses. As on the way up, so also on the way down: people trapped in poor housing or in poor neighbourhoods, or forced to 'filter' downwards from poor housing to poorer, may well suffer in their family aspirations and mobility, as well as the immediate discomforts of the poor housing.

These are commonplace observations, or uncertain hypotheses awaiting proper study. The conclusions for which our studies afford some more solid basis may be summed up as follows:

1. Housing is an important component of the system of social rewards. As long as society rewards its members unequally, according to their social contributions or any other criteria, housing conditions will continue to differ.
2. If housing differences are not allowed to occur in a market way, they will be produced by whatever method of allocation replaces the market. It is important that both housing policy and other social policies take account of this latent factor; if they fail to take account of it, their intended social effects may often be frustrated or distorted—as for example when a simple-minded policy of 'exactly equal housing for all' turns out in practice to increase housing and income inequalities.
3. The effects of housing circumstances on educational and social mobility within and between generations are variable, and are probably stronger in proportion as housing is poor, dense, and segregated.

CHAPTER 3

Towards a More Equitable Housing Policy in Socialist Eastern Europe

IN THE light of our study, the official claim that the Hungarian housing economy is a great socialist achievement appears—both before and after the reform of 1971—to be quite hollow. The actual achievements of housing policy are two:

1. A greater proportion of national income has gone to other capital investments than would have done so if housing had continued to be 'merchandise' which could attract its share of resources in a market way.
2. Rental apartments allocated nearly-free have become a substantial wage supplement, and their distribution has increased real income inequalities between social strata.

The purpose of this chapter is to sketch, if only in rough outline, some better principles and practice for a socialist housing economy.

Questions of principle

We observed earlier that the housing problem only becomes a social problem if people perceive unjust inequalities in the distribution of housing. We have also shown that some inequality is an unavoidable consequence of the social structure. The emergence of inequalities is necessary, but it is nonetheless necessary to combat them. It is the task of social policy to resolve this contradiction.

Arguing from these assumptions, A. Hegedus and M. Markus (1969) begin by distinguishing between concepts of 'basic' and 'differentiated' consumption. They think society should nominate a level of basic consumption, and assure it to everybody by taking the basic goods out of the market-place and distributing them directly. The market economy should then supply goods for 'differentiated' consumption—having been supplied with necessaries, people can then choose freely how to spend the 'unequal' part of their incomes. This general approach requires that the government designate the range of consumer goods to be regarded as 'basic' and distributed with strict equality.

Some such designation of basic rights to basic goods is common practice everywhere. It is not even particularly socialist. For a century or more all industrial countries have been developing public measures against starvation and physical misery. In the capitalist welfare states, people are assured of basic food and necessaries, medical care, and often social housing. As a matter of principle nobody is supposed to be in danger of starving, freezing, or doing without some minimal income and medical care. Historically the 'basic' provisions were originally set at the level of physical sustenance. Western experience has since proved that there is no absolute level of basic sustenance or income which can remove the social problem of poverty, because it is not basically a problem of sustenance, it is basically a problem of inequality. That has long been agreed by politically progressive sociologists in capitalist countries. (For examples, see Miller and Rein, 1966, and Rainwater, 1970.)

The need to define a level of basic consumption is thus beyond argument—but there can be plenty of argument about what the level should be, and which particular goods it should include. Hegedus and Markus do not nominate a specific basket of goods. They appear to think of it as a normative or moral task, to decide what minimum society *ought* to guarantee to its members. That does not help us much with the practical task, including the task of deciding how to treat housing. Should we decide, for example, that housing in its very nature is 'basic'? In that case it should be taken out of the market for direct distribution, and the policies analysed in this book should be ideal—which we believe they are not. Or should a certain minimum quality of housing be defined as basic and guaranteed as a right, while all housing above that standard is tolerated as market goods for differential consumption by those who can afford it? If that is the policy, *what* qualities should be defined as basic? Should they be qualities of house size, numbers of rooms and facilities, living density, urban access? Many houses with some of these qualities don't have others; criteria like 'living density' don't belong to the house but to the way it is used; so it looks very difficult to define either a 'basic consumer's entitlement' or a 'basic commodity' in any satisfactory, operational way.

In the study cited earlier, L. Rainwater (1970) criticizes physical definitions of sustenance or minimum welfare, and argues for a different test: the minimum living conditions in any society should be such as to allow everybody to be a full member of the society. For our purposes, that would include housing which allowed its residents to be full members of society. But, however valuable the concept of 'membership in the society' may be, especially as a corrective to narrower views of subsistence, it still does not tell us what specific housing quantities or qualities or distributions will serve the purpose in a practical, operational way.

We may come nearer to a practical solution by returning to an argument mentioned in Chapter 1. S. Greer (1966) argued that poor housing circumstances can function as links in a 'vicious circle' of causation which holds people in relative poverty or immobility, especially when various social disadvantages are superimposed, each making it harder for the people to escape the others. People trapped in that way are certainly hindered from living as full members of the society. We are therefore inclined to believe that *the first task of social policy in the housing economy should be to break that vicious circle*. The task for policy-oriented research would accordingly be to discover empirically the standards within which housing conditions do *not* perceptibly harm people's social opportunities or chances of mobility. It seems likely that a considerable range of housing styles and qualities will pass that test. If so, that range may be regarded as offering permissible diversity and differentiation for purposes of differential reward, and also to allow people with different needs and tastes to have some real options of life-style. On that basis, housing policy need not impose specific equalities; it must merely attack certain empirically-identifiable inequalities.

This returns us to the problem with which our study began. What is it that turns the housing question into a social problem? Is it the shortage of housing, or its distribution? We are now ready to answer: both. Hungary still does not have enough 'adequate' housing. It accordingly needs some housing additions and replacements. But no amount of physical improvement will rid the country of 'inadequate' housing unless the system of housing distribution is also working properly. The necessary basic minimum of housing for any family cannot be defined in physical terms, whether architectural or biological. It can only be defined in terms of current social relations and inequalities. The physical requirements change continuously —today's superior housing may be tomorrow's basic housing, today's slums may be rehabilitated socially as well as architecturally. The real requirement of 'basic' housing is that it should not trap people—people should be able to move from it to better housing *just as easily as they could move to that better housing from anywhere else.* That requires—broadly—two things: a housing stock without unacceptable extremes of slum housing or segregation; the efficient filtering of people through the housing stock, according to their real needs of means. Both those aims require some appropriate public action for their achievement; neither an open market, nor any other automatism, will by itself achieve them.

The public action needs to be different from that of the Hungarian government so far. Our analysis has shown that the attempt at deliberate social distribution of housing has in fact distributed it much as the market might have done, with some further effect of upsetting the intended distribution of real income. We now suggest that the state would serve its own declared social intentions better if it would build a more differentiated stock; permit more means of independent building; reduce segregation and facilitate 'filtering'; and charge market prices and rents to all who can afford them. In proposing that degree of 'market socialism' we are most emphatically not proposing any general increase in inequalities of income or living standards. On the contrary, we are proposing that the previous pattern of partly or wholly concealed benefits be brought into the open and incorporated plainly into the economic system and the visible distribution of income. If society wants two jobs to pay similar wages, and two families therefore to earn similar incomes, it should not then proceed to frustrate its own intentions by giving a large housing benefit to one but not the other, thus differentiating their real incomes substantially. If better-off families want better-than-average housing they should pay for it out of their better-than-average incomes. If those austere conditions should provoke second

thoughts about the desirable range of wage and income inequality, those arguments should be resolved on their merits,
not shelved in favour of covert 'wage supplements' conveyed
through the housing system. We are as interested as anybody in
reducing inequalities to the practicable minimum; but we think
that task will be done best if it is done with full awareness of the
real distributive effects of the relevant economic and social
policies.

To sum up: we believe that the state should do its best to
discover, by social research, the basic housing conditions which
are necessary if housing is to avoid contributing to the accumulation of social disadvantages. The housing resources which
pass through the national budget should then be directed to
seeing that housing of that necessary standard is available to all
who still lack it. That may be achieved by direct supplies of
social housing, or by other means. But the housing resources
that pass through the national budget, especially those that
convey elements of subsidy, should be directed to the social
groups who need them most. A first test of the social character of
any housing policy should be to ask who are the beneficiaries of
the resources centralized and redistributed by the state power.

Practical questions

It will be clear by now that we do not attach any intrinsic or
doctrinaire value either to market mechanisms or to administrative mechanisms of distribution. We do not believe that
either method, in itself, guarantees good social policies. We
think that useful function of the sociologist is to stimulate the
managers of the housing economy to design combinations of
market and non-market methods which will together channel
state housing services (and, where necessary, subsidies) to
groups who are disadvantaged in the labour market. In capitalist economies that often requires a substantial increase of state
intervention. In Hungarian circumstances, and elsewhere in
Eastern Europe, it requires some extension of market methods.
It also requires the redirection of both methods—it has been a
central contradiction within the Hungarian system that market
prices operate where there is most need for intervention and
subsidy, leaving masses of workers to build their own family
houses without assistance, while intervention and subsidy, in

the form of good state-owned apartments, go to the higher-income groups whose needs could be supplied most efficiently by market methods.

Practical reform should therefore be concerned first of all with the rental apartments the state builds, and the family houses the workers build. Together those two present the most immediate problems of both social and architectural policy.

The good state-built apartments should undoubtedly be marketed at economic rents. That will not affect their distribution much—most of those who get them by other means would be the ones to get them by market means. The managers of Hungarian housing policy have nevertheless stubbornly resisted any such introduction of a rental apartment market. During the drafting of the 1971 reform, several participants in the discussions proposed such a market, and the good reasons for it; but the law, as eventually enacted, included no steps in that direction. The managers' objections are ideological: how can the socialist state do market business in housing (they ask), when it has itself defined housing as a basic right of every citizen, *not* a market commodity? However ideologically pure, the objection is entirely hypocritical. The right to a new, rent-free apartment is not guaranteed by any law (despite frequent hints that it is). And it has no substance in practice. Moreover the authors of the fiction know it is a fiction. Nobody seriously expects the state to supply houses to country people, and the majority of townspeople, especially those with low incomes, have very remote prospects of state housing. Nor is socialism morally incompatible with market distribution of housing. Hungary has an extensive market in owner-occupied houses, and a state agency (the State Saving Bank) operates in it, building apartments for sale to private individuals. In the sector in which the State Saving Bank operates, moreover, the market functions badly because the State Saving Bank uses its monopoly of particular types of construction to maintain a seller's market. So it is indeed hypocritical to maintain that it would be 'anti-socialist' to charge market prices or rents for the high-quality apartments which the state supplies to people in the higher income groups. That housing supply has been a means of transferring resources from the society as a whole to its richest class. For housing and social reasons alike, it is an obvious candidate for market treatment—though the change-over might have to be slow, and might have to be accompanied by some changes in the wage structure, and in the organization of building construction.

There also need to be design changes. Merely to substitute market distribution for administrative distribution of the best new apartments would not in itself do anything to reduce segregation, or to help the social groups in most need of help with their housing. If new rental apartments are to be available to people with low incomes, there has to be some qualitative differentiation of the apartments built. As long as all new apartments are of uniform high quality the people with high incomes will get most of them under *any* system of distribution. So the architects must be persuaded to stop designing for that phantom 'standard person', and to design instead for a stratified market.

The main need is to differentiate the housing in our first housing class, the class of new state-built rental apartments. There are two ways to go—the class can be opened 'upwards' by producing some first-class grade A luxury apartments, or 'downwards' by producing first-class grade B apartments of lower quality. Both are capable of helping lower-income people, the first-class grade B apartments directly, and the first-class grade A apartments by their 'filtering' effect as they tempt sitting tenants to vacate standard apartments to people of lower income.

An opening 'upwards' is likely to be welcome to the designers and managers in the state bureaucracy. Architects take professional pride in designing good accommodation; the higher the standard, the happier they are. They see high standards as allowing professional versatility and fulfilment. They see cost constraints or 'utility standards', on the other hand, as hindrances imposed on their profession by outsiders. Besides the designers, the managers of the housing system could also suggest a number of reasons in favour of building bigger and better apartments. The apartments currently built look quite mean—especially in their numbers of rooms—by international standards. With so much substandard old housing already, the nation should not be adding *more* poor housing to the stock.

Higher standards would thus be welcomed inside the bureaucracy. But lower standards would not. The state architects and managers can be expected to oppose stubbornly any proposal to introduce first-class grade B class of lower-cost apartments. They will equate such proposals with a return to the 'austerity apartments' built through the 1950s which caused violent recoil, and were written off as failures, in both Hungary and Poland. We nevertheless recommend diversifying 'downwards' as well as 'upwards', for two general reasons. First, there are severe financial limitations on any 'upward' movement. In the early 1970s it already cost as much as 400,000 forints to produce the standard apartment, and that would already be hard to sell or rent at economic cost to the highest incomes in the national income structure. The absolute limit might be about half a million forints, corresponding roughly to a monthly rent of 3,000 forints—and even that might in practice require some state subsidy before the highest income groups could afford it. So the danger of diversifying 'upwards' is that it will merely increase the levels of subsidy paid to those who already have the highest incomes. If apartments of that quality, in any significant number, were 'auctioned' in an open market to the highest bidders, their prices and rents would be far below their production costs, given the going levels of personal incomes and building costs. So, even if the effect of establishing a 'luxury housing class' was the vacation of some standard apartments and the acceleration of filtering, which might benefit some members of all social strata, nevertheless, as a policy, it would be too expensive, and too uncertain in its distributive effects, to be adopted as the only or the main direction of housing differentiation. Differentiation 'downwards' is also necessary.

The need to produce lower-cost housing presents both architectural and economic problems. Architecturally, it is a mistake to equate all 'cheaper' possibilities with the unpopular postwar austerity housing. That particular housing was mostly cheapened by sticking to orthodox size and solid construction, with full construction costs, but leaving out a lot of necessary fittings and equipment and services. People understandably found it disagreeable to live in so it earned its bad reputation. But it might now be worth while to experiment with an opposite approach, i.e. one that put the necessary services and comforts into a cheaper structure with a shorter expected life.

To that proposal most state architects have a standard objection: they say that the costs of state construction are already pared to the bone, and that other, lighter types of construction would be no cheaper to build. We believe there is reason to doubt those assurances. Neither in design nor in building construction have there been any real incentives to economize. Reducing costs does not automatically appeal to designers who work in giant, bureaucratically organized design institutes, earning incomes which increase with the design costs. Moreover the architects often have to take many components as 'given'. Imported items, and the prefabricated components turned out by the housing factories, tend to be determined by others than the designers of the final buildings, who therefore have very little control over the costs of the buildings they design. The designs then pass to a construction industry which is strongly monopolistic, with little real competition between enterprises. All this leads us to suspect that the high building costs are unnecessary, and that their 'necessity' is a fiction concocted by the designing and building organizations. (Foreign experience of large-scale apartment-building, wherever it has been done by public authorities and by factory methods, has increasingly confirmed this view.) Accordingly, we believe that housing could be produced rather more economically if we designed differently, built lighter, shorter-lived structures, and made the building industry competitive.

Nevertheless a new class of cheaper, more modest housing could in turn become a social problem if its tenants could never move out of it. Basically it should be used and recognized as temporary housing, which people could leave after, say, five or ten years. It might even be expedient to emphasize its temporary character by demolishing or transporting houses which had served their purpose. Temporary houses should serve as 'housing trampolines', from which people could jump higher. They might thus rescue the sort of people who in 1970 were still living in basements and cellars, or in expensive sub-tenancies. (It was estimated that as much as a billion forints a year was being paid by sub-tenants to tenants of state-owned apartments.) There was mention of 'cheap' new housing in the Hungarian policy declaration of 1970, but the idea continued to be strongly resisted by state architects and housing managers and policy-makers, so early progress was not to be expected.

We continue to believe our proposals are right. To summarize: it is worth experimenting with two classes of new state housing. All first-class grade A housing should be distributed through the market, with the least practicable level of subsidy. Its main aim should be to attract the ambitions of the higher-income groups so that they will stop competing for the second class of state housing. That first-class grade B should be allowed where necessary to carry a little more subsidy than the first. It should be distributed by both market and administrative methods. Some of it should go out through the market, sometimes using devices of subsidy, regulation, or 'image-making' to direct it as far as possible to consumers with middle or low incomes. Meanwhile some of the same first-class grade B housing should be regarded as 'social' or welfare housing for administrative distribution, as a main resource of new housing for the lowest income groups. It need not, however, be their only resource. If credit arrangements were improved, and if the building industry was reorganized to allow more competitive enterprise, including building by small teams and independent tradesmen, then new supplies of market housing might well develop within the means of middle- and low-income buyers.

So much for reform and diversification within the state sector. The market sector also has its problems. The biggest volume of construction in this sector is the workers' construction of their own family houses. Strong 'urbanistic' and ideological prejudices prevail among the official and intellectual class in Hungary, and generally throughout Eastern Europe, against the independent family house that stands—usually only one storey high—on its own plot of land. These prejudices explain why, of all types of houses and modes of building, the building of family houses gets least official help or encouragement or financial or technical support.

Ideologists associate family houses with individualism and with the values of the *petite bourgeoisie*. In Hungary in the early 1960s there were vehement debates on the issue in the columns of the periodical *Reality* (*Valosag*). Family houses were condemned above all for 'privatizing' people. The accusation is scarcely worth contradicting: all our empirical knowledge goes to prove that family houses do not promote any more 'private mentality' than apartments or other housing forms do. The urbanistic objections were at least of a more rational kind. They were concerned with questions of urban density, the limited supply of building land, and problems of transport and services.

Whatever their force, they do not justify hypocrisies. The fact is that most of the urban working class is left to house itself by its own efforts. It is even denied much skilled or professional help—organized private building on any scale is forbidden, and state builders decline to build family houses, or allow them on state land. So the only housing form the workers *can* build, in law or in practice, is one or another simple kind of hut or bungalow on a piece of private ground. As long as the policies of government make that the workers' only resource, any official discrimination against those building forms and methods amount to discrimination against the already-disadvantages class which is forced to use them. So, even if we accept the urbanists' arguments about ideal urban forms (and they are widely disputed), we must still declare that the official dis-approval of family houses is anti-social.

We are also provoked to have some second thoughts about those same urbanists' claims to revolutionize housing and cities, and reduce social and economic costs, by using factory methods to construct multi-storey housing estates at high urban density, as the main housing form of the future. They have developed and applied those methods for many years now, with every official encouragement. There has been plenty of time to get over any 'growing pains' of the new building tech-nology. But we observe that the cheapest new housing in Hungary is still the family housing that the people build for themselves without much 'technology' at all.

PART II

URBAN PLANNING AND
SOCIAL STRUCTURE

CHAPTER 4

Urban Ecology and Social Inequality
—Introductory Remarks

IN previous chapters we have been dealing with the structure and dynamics of urban ecology by using the concept of housing class. That concept allows a 'macrosocial' understanding of the housing problem, where most sociological research into housing in the 1950s and 1960s was 'microsocial'. Much of the research of those decades was based on time and motion studies, time budget studies, design studies, and other approaches to the use of the house by its occupants. To caricature it somewhat, it discovered whether the power points in the kitchen and bathroom were correctly placed to plug in the washing machine. The work had its own practical importance, but it did not supply any basis for critical analysis of the housing system as a whole, or its relation to social structure. By contrast with that, the research reported above used the concept of housing class to allow the macrosocial analysis of housing distribution and mobility, and thus to connect urban ecology to social structure.

We now press that advantage further. The concept of housing class, and the research that it allows, may be the basis of significant developments of sociological theory. This book cannot hope to elaborate such theory, but we will now try to sketch some directions for it in terms of the data collected from our sample Hungarian cities of Pecs and Szeged.

J. A. Rex was the first to suggest housing class as a key concept for urban sociology (Rex, 1968; Pahl, 1968; Barbolet, 1969). His essay on the zones of transition defines such zones in terms of housing classes, and he studies urban mobility as a mode of competition for housing class positions—he goes as far as to call these competitions a form of class struggle. He is able to explain urban structures and processes in terms of the most important social conflicts, using the language of competition, monopoly, power, and so on; and the various urban zones can be differentiated in terms of their housing class composition.

In the analysis of urban structure we, as sociologists, are mainly interested to see how differently the various social strata are distributed in the cities, and to see whether or not their distribution creates disadvantages for some social groups and privileges for others. We begin with the hypothesis that the housing classes are distributed unevenly, and that their distribution is what chiefly determines the extent of any city's social segregation. The greater the segregation of housing classes from one another, the greater will be the segregation of the corresponding social strata; and the greater their segregation, the greater the differences and inequalities between them are likely to become. We find this hypothesis an attractive one because it helps to connect social segregation—the process which interests us most—to the processes of physical urban planning and development. Physical planning has the most direct effects on the uneven distribution of the housing classes, so the most important task for urban sociology is to discover the extent to which physical planning moderates or increases the inequality with which housing classes are distributed to urban zones.

Of course there are limits to the influence which urban planning can have on the segregational processes. Specific social systems and housing systems do a good deal to determine people's chances of social and housing mobility; and housing mobility is always limited in the short run by the nature and distribution of the existing housing stock, as well as by the quantity and quality of new building. But within those constraints urban planning can still be an important variable, with significant effects on processes of housing segregation, filtering, and mobility, and therefore also on social inequality and mobility. Some of our earlier research in Hungary seems to support this argument (see Szelenyi and Konrad, 1969). If urban planners concentrate particular housing classes in particular urban zones, they may well increase inequalities in access to housing. Planners should furthermore be aware that their work does not only affect people's access to housing; it can also affect their demands for housing and the values they put on it. If the most desirable housing is concentrated in exclusive areas, it is likely to increase its value as a status symbol, and increase people's desire to symbolize their status in their housing. It seems probable, for example, that one of the reasons why medium-sized co-operative apartment houses became a status symbol for intellectuals was the concentration of that class of housing in green-belt areas along with highly-valued villa housing. The spatial concentration of housing classes also has effects on the provision of infrastructure and services, and consequently on life-styles.

There is thus a kind of causal spiral, or accelerator: the more the urban planner concentrates the housing classes and segregates them from each other, the more differences are created between the life-styles of the social strata, and between their chances of housing mobility—so the more the segregation is reinforced.

Basically it is the differential chances of housing mobility which give the urban planner his power to influence the social structure. But that power may itself be limited and directed by particular housing policies. If it is policy to build particular types of housing, some of which require large sites or heavy constructional methods while others have quite different requirements, the planners may not have much real choice about the location of the housing types. If housing policy thus introduces housing classes of different character, and to some extent dictates their degree of segregation from each other, then planning policy can do comparatively little to increase or moderate the consequent social differences.

Thus we arrive at the decisive question: why are the various housing classes distributed so unevenly? It is obviously not from any single cause. Many processes in any given socio-economic system, together with features of both economic and natural geography, have helped to determine any given urban structure.

The fundamentals of economic geography show up in the uneven distribution of places of work. Work centres vary widely in size, location, and character. The types of work that concentrate in particular complexes are determined by the symbiotic relations of industries and institutions, past or present—a subject into which there has not been much research in urban sociology. Activities may locate together merely to share services like water supply, sewerage, transport; or they may have specific need of each other. Their need to communicate with each other may be such that modern means of communi-

cation at a distance are inadequate for them. This is specially
common in the tertiary sectors of the economy: universities and
research institutions cluster together; so do the head offices of
banks, insurance companies, and many commercial enterprises. But the different industries and institutions employ
different combinations of labour, so different employment
centres and complexes likewise have different composition of
labour. They therefore need to be, or tend to be, served by
residential areas of potentially different character. Urban
planners often intensify the potential differences by their zoning
policies. For example, different kinds of employment are
allowed different relations to residential areas: shops, offices,
and factories are zoned into concentrations of different size,
differently distanced from the housing of the people employed
in them. Cities whose planners concentrate their factory industries into one or a few central industrial zones have different
structures and residential arrangements from those which
locate factory industries at their outskirts. Except for their own
service needs, we have found most new housing estates to be
very short of employment, because of their strict residential
zoning; this may be one of the reasons why the new estates
rarely house many of the lowest income earners, who tend to
have the greatest need to live close to where they work.

The above is not meant as a general condemnation of zoning.
Zoning serves many rational purposes. But in its nature it tends
to put physical planning considerations, such as health and
safety, ahead of considerations of social solidarity; and in the
conscious pursuit of its good purposes it can have substantial
and often unintended effects on social structure and segregation.

Like economic geography, physical geography can also have
substantial effects on patterns of segregation. Those patterns
are influenced in obvious ways by the shape of the land, coast-
lines, river banks and so on, and local variations of micro-
climate. These help to determine where urban development
will go, and in some circumstances they affect the housing class
structure of particular areas. In capitalist societies, they exert
influence chiefly through the medium of land values: better and
worse living areas are available at different prices, which in turn
segregate the housing classes. It is worth emphasizing that the
effects of geography come about in different ways in socialist

countries, which have strict controls over the operation of their land markets. Most land is distributed administratively, by planning decision rather than by market competition. Zoning policies are accordingly more important than ever. Through most of Eastern Europe there has nevertheless continued to be strong differentiation and segregation in the distribution of housing classes. It would take further—and perhaps difficult—research to decide whether the segregation would have been greater or less under the operation of a market system.

Within this social, economic, and geographical framework—a framework set mainly by forces operating outside the sphere of urban planning—urban planning does still possess a certain autonomy, or independent influence. Most of that influence flows from decisions to concentrate and segregate the housing classes, or mix them more closely together. Our early research in Hungary (see Szelenyi and Konrad, 1969) suggested two disturbing things. First, the urban planners were generally unaware of the important social consequences of their policies. Second, most of their decisions were in the direction of increasing the extent and scale of segregation, and the social inequalities which follow from it.

The faster the cities grow, the greater is the tendency to create zones of homogeneous housing class composition. If large quantities of new housing have to be produced quickly, and if it is assumed that that can only be achieved by the use of large-scale industrial technology, then the planners are likely to look for large vacant sites, and fill them quickly with standardized types of housing. By those means cities do not grow organically; they grow by a series of cataclysmic changes. If those changes include the concentration of the newest and best housing—or the housing perceived as best, or available on the best terms—in large homogeneous zones, there may also be drastic effects on older urban areas. Those older, more mixed, more 'organic' districts may have their morale destroyed as their more successful residents leave, less successful residents come, and the old areas begin to confer low status on the residents who remain. 'Downward filtering' of the housing in a social sense is often accompanied by physical deterioration. Thus the high-status homogeneity and segregation on the newly built areas tends to impose a corresponding low-status homogeneity and segregation on the older areas. If those old areas come to be seen as 'bankrupt estates', and if the pressure for massive housing construction continues, then policies of urban renewal may also be affected, as large areas of the degraded old districts attract the bulldozer, and large-scale industrialized methods of building replacement. The damaging and homogenizing effects of that approach to renewal have been well researched in the United States and elsewhere (Anderson, 1964, Gans, 1959, 1965; Greer, 1966). Thus homogeneous zoning and segregation in new urban areas can spread its effects to old areas as well, to increase differentiation and inequality throughout the social ecology of the city.

These assumptions, derived from earlier investigations of new Hungarian housing estates, had a good deal to do with the choice of the two cities of Pecs and Szeged as sites of our survey, upon which this book is based. Those two differed in ways which allowed contrasting tests of our assumptions about planning and its social implications. Pecs had grown rapidly in population, area, and building development through the post-war decades. Moreover, it had grown from an old centre which was so constricted that the pressures on it produced something of a crisis, and forced a resort to new areas for development. We therefore expected to find the effects outlined above evident in its development. Szeged presented a double contrast. Its population was stagnant for ten years from 1945; and towards the end of the last century, provision had been made for a town centre which could function as the centre for one or two hundred thousand people. The development of Szeged should accordingly have been able to take more organic forms.

In those contrasting conditions we set out to see whether the facts would confirm our theoretical expectations about the effects of housing segregation on social processes and inequalities. Our assumptions were roughly as follows: the uneven distribution of housing classes, with segregation of class from class, tends to segregate different life-styles, and increase inequalities between them. Zones inhabited by different housing classes tend to attract different networks of institutions and services. That happens automatically in market conditions, to the extent that commercial and cultural and service industries can locate themselves where there is high consumer demand. In capitalist conditions those same favoured areas are often favoured with better public services as well, because, besides their consumer demand, they also have a better tax base and more collective bargaining power.

Similar effects occur in socialist conditions, despite the weakness or absence of many of the market processes. If districts have different housing classes and social strata, they generate different needs under non-market conditions as well as under market conditions. They also generate different capacities to get what they want, by fighting or bargaining or any other means. People in middle-class districts have more contacts, they have more of the skills required in bureaucratic negotiation, they have better access to many sources of information. So a segregated middle-class district will often attract a department store before a working-class district does, and it will often get a larger share of the urban services and infrastructure that its residents want. Those advantages will be superimposed on the housing advantages such districts already possess. Meanwhile segregated working-class districts will suffer the corresponding disadvantages; their life-style and opportunities of mobility will suffer accordingly; so will their individual and collective capacities to do anything effective about the inequalities from which they suffer. In such districts the physical deterioration of the housing runs parallel to changes in the composition of the residents, leaving generally lower incomes, and declining standards in important local services and institutions, especially the schools. Maria Pap and Csaba Pléh (1972) found some very important results in a study they made of the use of language by pre-school children of various social backgrounds, living in areas of various character. They found that, in Budapest, the use of language is not generally class-specific, i.e. there is no significant difference in the way the Hungarian language is used by a child from a working-class background and a child from an intellectual background. But those results are from socially mixed districts of the capital city. Where the housing classes are segregated, there are noticeable differences. If they live in segregated districts of different character, the children tend to use the language differently. A working-class child from a segregated district is more likely to use the 'restricted codes' of working-class language than is the working-class child from a socially integrated district. Segregated working-class districts, soon identified as slums, create their own unique subculture. That subculture joins (often) with official neglect to cause many local institutions to deteriorate. The causation is then circular—but the circle was usually set in motion by the segregation of the district.

It was with these models and expectations in mind that we designed our study of the urban structure and ecology of Pecs and Szeged. The following chapters report the findings of the study. Those are then followed by an attempt to develop, on the basis of those findings, a general theory of urban development applicable to Eastern Europe at large.

CHAPTER 5

Ecological Structure of Two Hungarian Cities

THE following chapters deal with the relationship between the ecology and the social structure of the cities of Pecs and Szeged. As indicated earlier, our survey of the two cities was designed to find out how the unequal distribution of social privileges and disadvantages arising from the differentiation of socialist society was related to the ecology of the social groups concerned, i.e. to their spatial distribution and mobility.

We knew before we started that the facts would not agree with the manifest aim of the relevant public policies. The manifest aim of housing policy, planning policy, social policy, and of modern democratic urban development in general is to reduce any inequalities which arise from spatial or other urban causes, and specifically to do away with social segregation and promote social integration instead. To explain inconsistencies between these policy aims and their actual effects it would not be sufficient merely to map the offending distributions. We needed to develop a dynamic model capable of explaining the migrations and social processes which were frustrating the official aims. For that purpose it was necessary to find out how the two main modes of official intervention, namely housing policy and urban planning, actually interacted with the spontaneous processes of migration and settlement. There could be direct effects of intervention, intended and unintended; there could be reactions from the public which might modify the policies or their effects; there could be interactions between the various lines of intervention. There might also, of course, be some continuing effects of past historical causes, but these were dwindling; the condition of the cities was increasingly the achievement of the branches of government responsible for urban planning and development, land policy, housing policy and production, housing credit, and housing allocation. If that complex of related activities was not achieving enough of its aims, it must be in need of some better means of understanding how its interventions were acting and reacting with the spontaneous urban processes to produce unsatisfactory effects. Modern urban planning is a species of social planning. To be effective it must have a good capacity to forecast the significant social consequences of alternative policies of investment, distribution, and regulation. It was to an improvement of the forecasting capacity that we hoped our research would contribute.

Urban zones and the social processes within them

The following analysis was designed to discover the social characteristics of the zoning systems of the two cities. We wanted to discover any relations between the physical and functional characteristics of the zones, and their demographic and social composition. If zones were ranked in a hierarchy of physical characteristics, would they show any corresponding hierarchy of social rank?

We were thus looking for measures and mechanisms of social segregation. In line with that purpose, we took care to define the zones by characteristics other than their social composition. They were defined instead by reference to three main factors: their types of housing stock, their economic and institutional functions, and their historical character as evidenced partly by their date of construction and partly by inhabitants' perceptions. Social characteristics, including the composition of the population, were deliberately ignored, because they were what the analysis was designed to discover. To put it more formally: in this investigation we treated zones defined by their architecture and economic function as independent variables, and the social characteristics of those zones as dependent variables.

In choosing the zones and their boundaries we relied on the opinions of expert informants, drawn from city council officials (including the chief architects of the two cities), university lecturers who knew the cities well, and older inhabitants of the cities. We personally inspected the boundaries suggested by those advisers to make sure that they met the criteria listed above.

With those aids we arrived at a two-level system of zones for Pecs and Szeged. In each city we first defined a large number of individual zones. These were then grouped into five abstract classes—city centre, transitional zone, mixed industrial–residential areas, outer suburbs of family houses, and new multi-storey housing estates—which together suffice to describe the ecological structure of any substantial town in Hungary, including Budapest. These five, presently elaborated to six, became the basic zones of our study. Some of them had different acreage in the two cities. In more detail, they were determined as follows:

City centre

Ignoring administrative boundaries wherever necessary, the city centre was defined functionally as the central area in which are located the institutions which satisfy city-wide needs, plus the area from which those institutions are in ten or fifteen minutes' walking distance. In both cities the centre so defined could be divided into a central part and an outer ring. The central part is characterized by streets with continuous building, mainly row houses, most of several storeys. It usually coincides with the historical nucleus and is bounded by the remains of the old city walls. The outer ring is more mixed architecturally, but still has to be regarded as part of the centre because it contains a number of city-wide institutions.

Transitional zone

By this we understand an area of historical city, beyond the city walls and the outer ring of the centre, which lies between the centre and the modern industrial and residential areas. The zone of transition is characterized by mixed building forms, including detached and semi-detached housing and some continuous row housing, and it has a mixture of residential, industrial, and commercial uses. The architectural and functional mixtures vary so much that we divided the zone into two more homogeneous subdivisions, defined chiefly by the physical state of the housing:

First Transitional Zone. Areas with good housing standards. In Pecs, these include many of the best villa-style family houses and some co-operative apartment houses of good quality; the zone includes an attractive area of hillside with a garden suburb and new co-operative apartments. Similarly in Szeged, this zone includes areas where recent building has created a mixture of good family houses and good medium-sized apartment houses.

Second Transitional Zone.   Here are the inner areas of old, poor, and deteriorating housing, containing many village-style houses and much of the city's old single-storey multi-flat housing.

Mixed industrial–residential areas

Defining this zone presented some theoretical problems. In both cities, as in many other Hungarian cities, distinct industrial districts were established around the turn of the century when the growth of the cities was much slower. The factory areas were originally developed on open land 'out of town', but the cities have since expanded to surround them, or to take in the towns which had meanwhile developed around them. Consequently the old industries now mix with the family houses of the 1920s and the housing estates of the 1950s. Some of these mixtures are entirely surrounded by the expanding suburbs; others still reach to the periphery of urban development, and have room for some continuing industrial development. These characteristics prompted us to classify such areas in a zone of their own, rather than treating them as extensions of the transitional zone.

Outer suburbs of family houses

In the larger country towns in Hungary the transitional zones and the industrial–residential areas are often surrounded by an outer circle of settlement of predominantly suburban or village character. Various kinds of development have created these areas. There was some continuing 'suburban sprawl' of villa-style and cottage-style housing through the first half of the century. New areas of modest family housing have continued to develop with the extension of the cities' administrative boundaries. They include a good deal of working-class, cottage-style housing built under the new regime, some of it with aid or credit from state institutions, some by the labour of the occupiers themselves. This zone as a whole is characterized by single-storey family housing with private gardens, but its quality varies widely. Parts are truly suburban: the houses are in villa or cottage style, their gardens are used for gardening and relaxation, they are connected to good network services. Other parts are poorer and more village-like: they have fewer urban services, the houses are poorer and often older, vegetables grow and animals graze in their gardens.

New multi-storey housing estates

These are new estates of state-built and usually state-owned housing, in the form of multi-storey blocks of apartments of good quality, with full urban services. Szeged had one such estate, built in the 1960s; Pecs had two, one built in the 1950s and a second being finished at the time of our survey at the end of the 1960s.

Having defined the zones, we tested them for 'urban homogeneity', by which we chiefly meant homogeneity in the age and physical character of the housing they contained. On this premiss multi-storey housing should constitute the whole of the housing in the new housing estates, a majority of the housing in the city centre, and the largest category of housing in the first transitional zone. The second transitional zone should have most of the single-storey flats, with some also in the industrial–residential areas. Single-storey family houses should predominate in the outer residential circle. The figures, as shown in Table 5.1, confirm these assumptions well enough.

We also tabulated the age of the housing (Table 5.2). Table

TABLE 5.1
Distribution of families living in different housing types in the urban zones

Zone	% of multi-storey houses	% of single-storey apartment houses	% of single-storey family houses	Number in sample
City centre	69.1	21.7	9.2	544
Transitional zone I	38.1	31.0	30.1	186
Transitional zone II	18.0	46.1	35.9	357
New multi-storey housing estates	100.0	0.0	0.0	191
Mixed industrial–residential areas	21.7	35.3	43.0	595
Outer suburbs of family houses	7.1	13.6	79.3	397

TABLE 5.2
Age of the housing in the urban zones

Zone	% before 1920	% 1920–1944	% after 1945	Number in sample
City centre	62.5	16.3	21.2	448
Transitional zone I	34.0	41.2	24.8	169
Transitional zone II	59.8	28.3	12.9	321
New multi-storey housing estates	0.0	0.0	100.0	191
Mixed industrial–residential areas	45.9	28.0	26.1	542
Outer suburbs of family houses	18.2	45.8	36.0	375

5.2 needs to be read with some care. The age of housing is often a good index to its condition—both its physical condition and its 'morale'. On that assumption the table confirms some differences between the zones and some homogeneity within them. But age is not a uniform index of present-day quality or condition. For example, the city centre and the second transitional zone have similar proportions of old housing. The old housing in the city centre, inherited from the old *bourgeoisie*, tends to be spacious, well-kept, and adequately modernized. Much of it in both cities is officially perceived as possessing historical importance. By contrast, housing over fifty years old in the second, poorer, transitional zone was smaller and poorer when it was built and has usually deteriorated since. The industrial–residential areas also have high proportions of older housing. It was built as workers' housing during the first surge of industrialization in Hungary, from about 1900 on to about 1920. Between the wars, and after the Second World War, these areas saw some continuing construction, mostly of modest family houses. Larger proportions of new housing construction between the wars went to two other zones. One was the outer suburbs, where public servants, *petite bourgeoisie*, and workers with secure incomes graduated to suburbia all over urban Hungary through those decades. They were joined there—then and since —by immigrants from rural Hungary, that is to say by those who were able to sell their village properties for enough to enable them to buy into the urban housing market. As the older industrial residential areas ran out of available land between the wars and after, municipal authorities co-operated to develop this outer suburban circle of purely residential character. The other area of intense housing construction in the 1930s was the first transitional zone. Its better parts were handy to the city centre, with the environmental attractions of hillside or riverside. Villas and apartment blocks were built there, of better quality and with better facilities and services than were available in the outer suburban developments of the same years. After the war these areas continued to attract some of the best new housing, in the form of co-operative apartment blocks of good quality and medium density. Meanwhile the most spectacular achievement of the post-war years has been the construction of the new high-density estates of large multi-storey apartment buildings. They were built in new areas, on open land, for reasons described elsewhere (Szelenyi and Konrad, 1969). Their construction has modified fundamentally the ecological structure of the pre-war Hungarian cities. In that traditional structure the best housing in each of the better housing classes was to be found in the city centre. Some of the best housing has since gone to the first transitional zone, and some of it to the new multi-storey estates at the urban outskirts, so that in their residential arrangements the cities have become twinned or multi-nucleic, with more than one focus of quality and prestige. At the same time the largest quantity of new private development has continued to occur in the outer-suburbs. It includes some planned estates of workers' housing, and rather more 'suburban sprawl' of new family housing built privately, often by the working-class families themselves.

Just as the age and type of housing differs from zone to zone, so does its ownership. In the city centre 78.4 per cent of the housing is owned by the state, partly because of the importance of the area and partly because of the number of privately owned multi-storey buildings which were nationalized. In the new multi-storey estates about half the housing remains in state ownership and the other half belongs, as co-operative housing, to its occupiers. In the first transitional zone a third of the housing is owned by the state, 45 per cent by the occupiers, and 22 per cent by other private individuals. In the second, deteriorating, transitional zones only 17 per cent is state owned; half the housing belongs to its occupiers and a third to other private individuals. State ownership is higher in the industrial–

residential areas, especially among the single-storey apartment houses; and it is lowest (at 8 per cent) in the outer suburbs where three-quarters of the family houses are owned by the families who live in them.

It has already been shown that the new multi-storey estates, the city centre, and the first transitional zone contain most of the higher housing classes. By contrast, the second transitional zone, the industrial–residential areas, and the outer suburbs contain most of the housing of poorer quality. One good indicator of housing quality is the masonry itself: in the areas of high status, mud-walled houses are rare or non-existent, while in areas of low status they are usual. In the second transitional zone a third of the houses have mud walls; so do 23 per cent of houses in the outer suburbs, and 14 per cent in the industrial–residential areas.

Another important item of housing quality is the presence or absence of plumbing and standard network services (Tables 5.3 and 5.4).

TABLE 5.3
Distribution of houses with plumbing facilities in the urban zones

Zone	% with bathroom and all facilities	% with WC but no bathroom	% without any facilities	Number in sample
New multi-storey housing estates	98.0	2.0	—	191
City centre	61.2	19.3	19.5	544
Transitional zone I	62.4	28.6	9.0	180
Transitional zone II	33.2	26.3	40.5	358
Mixed industrial– residential areas	40.8	21.2	38.0	596
Outer suburbs of family houses	48.0	17.7	34.3	400

Of the network services we believe that water and electricity are the most important, at least to public health. Because 98.7 per cent of houses have electricity, access to piped water could well serve as a sufficient indicator of housing quality in the various zones (Table 5.5).

It is perhaps in families' access to these standard facilities

TABLE 5.4
Distribution of houses with network services in the urban zones

Zone	water, gas electricity	water electricity	gas electricity	electricity only	none	Number in sample
New multi-storey housing estates	97.0	3.0	—	—	—	192
City centre	68.4	20.5	1.5	9.6	—	511
Transitional zone I	32.1	55.1	0.5	12.3	—	190
Transitional zone II	10.3	35.0	2.7	51.0	1.0	360
Mixed industrial–residential areas	8.0	42.0	1.7	46.6	1.7	599
Outer suburbs of family houses	2.5	48.7	—	44.8	4.0	402

TABLE 5.5
Distribution of houses supplied with piped water in the urban zones

Zone	% with piped water	% without piped water	Number in sample
New multi-storey housing estates	100.0	—	192
City centre	88.1	11.9	551
Transitional zone I	87.4	12.6	190
Transitional zone II	45.3	54.7	360
Mixed industrial–residential areas	50.1	49.9	599
Outer suburbs of family houses	50.8	49.2	402

and services that the housing inequalities are most dramatic. Living standards and life-styles depend in many ways on such services—yet, at the extremes, 98 per cent of families in the new multi-storey estates have all the services, while only 28 per cent of families in the second transitional zone have all of them. Everyone in the best zone has running water; less than half the households in the worst zone have it. If it is permissible to talk of 'underdeveloped regions', then it is time we talked just as urgently of 'underdeveloped zones' within the cities.

It is on information of this general kind that democratizing, equalizing strategies of urban development need to be based. That is partly because the physical and spatial inequalities are important in themselves, and need to be reduced. But it is even more important to know their social distribution, and how they relate to inequalities of status and income, if strategies of equalization are to have their intended effects and not be ineffective or even counter-productive. Accordingly, it is with the social distribution of the physical and spatial inequalities that the following section is concerned.

The social composition of the urban zones

We have at our disposal a wide range of data about the social and demographic composition of the various zones. The social 'rank' of the zones, and the degree of segregation of particular social strata in and between the zones, can be measured by use of the variables shown in Table 5.6, 5.7, and 5.8.

TABLE 5.6
Educational qualifications of heads of households in the urban zones

Zone	Grades 1–7	Grades 8–11	At least matric.	Number in sample
New multi-storey housing estates	14.7	32.4	52.9	191
City centre	31.3	25.6	43.1	550
Transitional zone I	33.2	31.1	35.7	190
Transitional zone II	52.1	30.9	17.0	350
Mixed industrial–residential areas	53.1	33.4	13.5	593
Outer suburbs of family houses	53.4	34.0	12.6	399

TABLE 5.7
Occupations of heads of households in the urban zones

Zone	Intellectual	Other white-collar workers	Skilled blue-collar workers	Unskilled blue-collar workers	Number in sample
New multi-storey housing estates	22.5	28.3	31.2	18.0	191
City centre	17.2	30.8	20.5	31.5	511
Transitional zone I	14.7	25.2	19.6	40.5	190
Transitional zone II	6.2	17.2	25.4	51.2	361
Mixed industrial–residential areas	3.5	14.0	27.4	55.1	598
Outer suburbs of family houses	4.0	16.4	25.7	53.9	400

TABLE 5.8

Occupations of heads of households in zones of high and low status

Zones of high status: new multi-storey housing estates, city centre, and transitional
zone I.
Zones of low status: transitional zone II, mixed industrial–residential areas,
outer suburbs of family houses.

Occupational status	% in zones of high status	% in zones of low status	Number in sample
Intellectual	77.0	23.0	216
Other white-collar	58.2	41.8	465
Skilled blue-collar	35.7	64.3	583
Unskilled blue-collar	27.8	72.2	1024

To simplify further: 70 per cent of intellectual and white-collar workers live in zones of higher status and 30 per cent in zones of lower status. For blue-collar workers those figures are exactly reversed: 70 per cent live in zones of lower status and 30 per cent in zones of higher status.

We conclude, from the analysis so far, that the degree of segregation of our cities is measurable. It is also clear that all the measured social and spatial advantages tend to be super-imposed on one another to increase the privilege of the privileged, while the corresponding disadvantages go together to worsen the situation of the disadvantaged. The higher social classes with the higher status and the better educational qualifications are situated in the better zones of the city; the lower social classes with lower status and less education tend to live in the poorer zones.

When we turn from the social composition of the zones to their demographic composition, we find less differences between them—the better zones do not necessarily have the youngest, most dynamic population. The youngest zones are the new multi-storey housing estates where 78 per cent of the heads of households are under 45, and the outer suburbs where 45 per cent of heads of households are under 45. The population is older in the city centre, and oldest in the transitional zones where two-thirds of the heads of households are over 45.

The areas of new building have a younger population because they are built specifically for young families. Families with children under 18 years of age make up 75 per cent of the households in the new multi-storey estates, 51 per cent of those in the outer suburbs, 44 per cent of those in industrial–residential areas, 41 per cent of those in the city centre, and 35 per cent of those in the transitional zones. So also with the age of the children: there are small children in two-fifths of the families in the new multi-storey estates, one-fifth in the outer suburbs, and one-tenth in the city centre and transitional zones.

It is obvious from the above that the cities tend to be older towards their centres and younger towards their outskirts. In a number of the zones, fortunately, the social and demographic segregations are not superimposed on each other. But they are superimposed at the extremes. The youngest people and highest status are found together in the new multi-storey estates. The oldest and most disadvantaged are to be found in the second transitional zone, where the accumulated segregations encourage the further deterioration of the housing, and the status and age structure of the people.

Having observed where the various categories of people live, with what advantage and disadvantage, we may now explore the dynamic processes which distribute particular groups to particular zones.

Table 5.9 shows how our sample population was distributed in the urban zones. That picture can be further simplified to say that two-fifths of the families live in zones of high status, and three-fifths in zones of low status. What are the factors that determine which families go to which zones?

TABLE 5.9
Distribution of population in the urban zones

Zone	%	Number in sample
New multi-storey housing estates	8.4	192
City centre	24.1	552
Transitional zone I	8.2	189
Transitional zone II	15.7	361
Mixed industrial–residential areas	26.1	595
Outer suburbs of family houses	17.5	402

We can begin by asking which housing was obtained by administrative allocation, and which by one or another market mechanism (Table 5.10). 'Administrative allocation' means

TABLE 5.10
How housing was obtained in the urban zones

Zone	% by administrative allocation	% from the market	Number in sample
New multi-storey housing estates	100	00.0	192
City centre	80.4	19.6	552
Transitional zone I	30.6	69.4	189
Transitional zone II	17.2	82.8	361
Mixed industrial–residential areas	35.6	64.4	598
Outer suburbs of family houses	8.2	91.8	402

allocation of state-built or state-owned housing by municipal authorities. Although co-operative apartments are privately owned we include them in this category because the same municipal authorities allocate them. 'From the market' means housing bought or rented from private individuals, or built by its occupiers, or inherited.

The system of allocation which operated in Hungary until the summer of 1971 provided that those who got housing by administrative allocation from local authorities got it virtually free. There was no capital payment, and the monthly rent was too low even to cover maintenance costs—it was perhaps a tenth of the notional market rent, including the black market rent for the same apartments. Those who were allocated state-built co-operative housing paid a fee for it, but still got it far below cost. Since the alternative to state allocation was to build privately or buy a house from another private citizen, at full building cost or market price, there developed acute competition for the limited supplies of the state housing, which was not only cheaper, but tended also to be of the best quality. How could these limited supplies be allocated? Not surprisingly, they tended to go to the applicants who had high social status or special merit or 'social usefulness'. The previous chapters noticed the relation between housing allocation and social status. In Table 5.11 we show what percentage of the various occupational groups managed to get the free or near-free state housing.

Those with higher status and income thus had better access to the free state housing. What is rather more surprising is that,

TABLE 5.11
How occupational groups obtained their housing
(This table excludes housing exchange and purchase of co-operative housing)

Occupational status	% allocated free state housing	% obtained by other means:		Number in sample
		built	bought	
Intellectuals and high bureaucrats	39.0	23.0	38.0	215
Other white-collar workers	28.0	28.0	44.0	458
Skilled blue-collar workers	23.0	34.0	43.0	575
Semi-skilled and unskilled blue-collar workers, retired workers	19.0	36.0	45.0	1021

even if they were forced to build, buy, or exchange their housing, they still managed to pay comparatively less for it, on average, than poorer people did. Table 5.12 shows the average prices paid in the different zones by those who had to pay at all.

TABLE 5.12
What families paid for their houses in the urban zones

Zone	% who paid less than 20,000 forints	% who paid 20–50,000 forints	% who paid 50–100,000 forints	% who paid more than 100,000 forints	Number in sample
New multi-storey housing estates	87.5	12.5	0.0	0.0	80
City centre	46.0	25.5	16.0	12.5	64
Transitional zone I	23.2	8.2	26.8	41.8	56
Transitional zone II	12.2	23.2	38.3	26.3	92
Mixed industrial–residential areas	31.0	19.3	25.7	24.0	187
Outer suburbs of family houses	6.1	15.4	33.3	45.2	228

People with lower incomes who got poor housing in poor districts of the city typically paid more for it than richer people paid for better housing in better districts. The summary Table 5.13 dramatizes the discrimination.

The mobility of the population from zone to zone is largely

TABLE 5.13
Prices paid for housing by families who did not get allocated free housing

Zone	% who paid less than 50,000 forints	% who paid more than 50,000 forints	Number in sample
Three best zones	72.0	28.0	200
Three worst zones	35.0	65.0	507

determined by three things: (1) the working of the housing economy: (2) the strategy and practice of urban development; and (3) the differing demands, ambitions, and preferences of the families who make up the various social groups.

We have analysed the working of the housing economy. Its mechanisms tend to favour people of higher status and income, and locate them in the better zones of the city, namely the city centre, the better transitional zone of co-operative medium-density housing, and the new multi-storey estates. By contrast, most working-class families have to build their own houses, using their own and their friends' or relations' labour. They do not build their own family houses because they find the idea attractive, but rather because they are forced to do so. They have slender chances of being allocated free state housing or low-priced co-operative housing. They rarely inherit much, so not many have enough capital to buy housing, or to hire professional labour to build for them. So they build for themselves, at the rate at which their current income allows. Many build a room or two, then move in and continue building bit by bit as they earn the price of the minimum materials. Finishing the family house can take ten years or more.

This economic necessity is of fundamental importance. It explains why the most energetic and economically-minded working-class families go in such large numbers to the outer suburban areas, and to any unbuilt land to be found in the old industrial districts. There, some discriminations continue. They may have to pay market prices for land, as the luckier inhabitants of state housing do not. If they are able to borrow at all they get less credit at higher rates of interest than do the middle-class purchasers of co-operative apartments. But at least, in those unprivileged zones, they get a degree of freedom to provide for themselves the basic accommodation which the state is unlikely to provide for most of them in any near future—if ever.

Thus a great many of the families who need new housing are driven to the comparatively cheap suburban allotments. That pressure is reinforced by the dominant urban planning policies. For technical, economic, organizational, and philosophical reasons, the planning authorities have not been able to resolve the reconstruction problems of the deteriorating transitional zones. So they stick to the easier business of subdividing open land at the outskirts of the city, and leave most working-class families to build there for themselves.

There remains an even poorer housing class, too poor or disadvantaged to have the option of building for themselves. They may lack money, health, strength, or family labour. Twenty per cent of the families in Pecs and Szeged were living in houses defined as unhealthy. Most of those are old houses, long overdue for reconstruction, in the deteriorating transitional zones and the industrial districts.

To understand how the most disadvantaged people are 'locked into' deteriorating areas which are systematically deprived of building resources, it is necessary to understand the double competition for urban position, and for investment funds. For this purpose we must begin by remembering that our own classifications of higher and lower standards are merely relative. The best urban zones are still not perfect—and more important, they are not entirely satisfactory to their residents. In the superior downtown areas of the city centre and the better transitional zone there are still some poor and unhealthy houses, whose occupants want to move to the outer suburbs if that is the best move available to them. Thirty seven per cent of the intellectuals and white-collar workers in the survey were dissatisfied with the condition of the buildings they lived in. Almost a tenth of the intellectual families lived at a density of two persons per room, or worse. More than a tenth of them lived in flats without bathrooms, and another tenth lived in lodgings or co-tenancies. Fifteen per cent were so dissatisfied with their housing that they wanted to move to somewhere better. And, although intellectuals and white-collar and skilled workers have better chances of getting state housing, their advantages are only relative, and there is never enough state housing for them all. A number of them therefore go to the outer suburban areas, which are at least young and healthy and dynamic: even if somewhat backward or unsophisticated from an urban point of view, they are not districts in decline.

That leaves the deteriorating transitional zone as the real problem area, where physical and social disadvantages most clearly reinforce each other. A number of housing and planning policies converge to intensify the disadvantages of these areas:

1. Although these areas have the oldest and poorest housing in the most urgent need of replacement or reconstruction, nevertheless all new state-directed housing investment goes to open land outside the settled areas.

2. Location has no official value, so well-placed urban land is not recognized as having special value. A high proportion of central city land is owned by the state. The policy that housing and land should not be market commodities has meant that a great deal of this centrally-placed residential land is leased for next to nothing, and privately-owned land in the same areas is taxed and rent-controlled like land anywhere else, regardless of its advantageous location. It follows that neither state investors nor private home-builders have much incentive to use central land more efficiently. Throughout the city centre and the adjoining transitional zones it is possible to find many patches of under-occupied land where poor or valueless buildings, of residential and other kinds, continue to take up a lot of valuable space.

3. The areas to which new housing investment goes instead are planned and developed to be extremely homogeneous in terms of ownership and of the age and type and standard of housing. Specifically, (i) In the suburban areas of single-storey family houses there are no state or privately-owned flats for those with individual needs, and no apartments of higher value to attract people of higher status. (ii) Neither in the multi-storey housing estates nor in the outer suburban areas are there housing mixtures like these which can be found over much of Western Europe—mixtures which allow families with children to find terrace houses, 'garden apartments', or other medium-density housing alongside developments of higher and lower density for households of different ages and needs and tastes.

4. The new housing developments never include any housing of lower quality and cost which might allow poorer families from the deteriorating slums to move to new areas of better physical and social character. If a new area has similar quality and cost all over, it tends to follow that its space will be competed for by similar people from a single social class, and the better-off competitors will win, and move in. They are likely to meet richer or poorer or older neighbours only if richer or poorer or smaller—or appropriately *different*— housing is there to attract such diverse people. The only way to achieve a social mix in new housing developments is to offer varieties of housing types and standard—and socialist planners have so far found that politically and ideologically difficult to do.

The above factors combine to locate most new housing development at the outskirts of the city. Young families with higher incomes go to the state-owned multi-storey estates; young families with lower incomes buy or build family houses on the outer-suburban subdivisions. Among those who are left behind in the city centre and the deteriorating transitional zones, many of the poorer households stay only because they are too old to move, or because they cannot afford to. As those who can get out do so, the average status and wealth and youth and vigour of the remaining community declines, and so also (by public policy) does the physical fabric in which they live, each process reinforcing the other.

How are patterns of mobility related to the changing character of the zones (Table 5.14)? In both cities there has been considerable population growth. Immigrants to the cities have tended to concentrate in three of the zones. Intellectual immigrants are mostly of urban origin, and tend to move into the new housing estates. Most working-class immigrants are of rural origin. Those who had rural homes to sell, to raise some capital, were likely to buy or build family houses when they moved to town. Those who lacked resources to buy or build new houses for themselves, and could not get state-allocated housing either, might buy an old house in the older transitional area, or might become lodgers with friends or relatives, or with old people offering accommodation in return for care. Generally the poorer immigrants tended to move into the older areas of the second transitional zone.

TABLE 5.14
Zone-to-zone mobility, by urban zones

Zone	Number of families in sample	% of the sample	% who lived in the same house since 1950 or moved within the zone	% who moved from a different zone of the same city since 1950	% who moved from another town since 1950	% who formed the family in this zone
New multi-storey housing estates	192	8.4	11.0	68.1	16.7	4.2
City centre	552	24.1	38.2	37.8	17.2	6.8
Transitional zone I	189	8.2	25.0	43.2	26.5	5.3
Transitional zone II	361	15.7	44.0	17.0	26.0	13.0
Mixed industrial–residential areas	598	26.1	45.0	26.9	19.2	9.8
Outer suburbs of family houses	402	17.5	23.0	34.4	33.6	9.0
All together	2294	100.0				

The immobile households—those who have not moved for eighteen years or more—tend to be found in three zones. One is the city centre where many of the old *bourgeoisie*, the intelligentsia, and the white-collar workers have stayed on in their old homes. Another is the industrial–residential zone where numbers of managers, technicians, and some skilled blue-collar workers have been content to stay on in their old homes. The third is the older transitional zone, where a large number of pensioners retired from blue-collar work have stayed. These three are the zones of comparatively stable population. The proportion of old inhabitants is naturally lowest where there has been most recent urban development, in the new multistorey estates and in the first transitional zone. These two also have the highest proportion of migrants from other zones of the same city, while the outer suburbs—the other fast-growing zone—attracts more of the rural immigrants.

The zonal mobility of the social classes shows some trends over time. As the general housing situation improved, there were effects on the opportunities of all sections of the population. Throughout the two decades preceding the survey, the

proportion of 'old inhabitants' in the city centre population fell
7 per cent, in the first transitional zone 16 per cent, in the second
transitional zone 27 per cent, and in the industrial–residential
areas 6 per cent. It is of interest to see who stayed, and who
moved where. Table 5.15 classifies families by their *per capita*
earnings: 'high incomes' represent the 55.3 per cent of the
population with more than 1,000 forints of income per head,
and 'lower incomes' represent the 44.7 per cent with less than
1,000 forints per head. The urban zones are grouped into 'high
status areas' and 'low status areas' as in earlier tables. The
overall effect of these movements includes some net improvement—the 16 per cent who moved 'upwards' outnumbered the
11.7 per cent who moved 'downwards'. But both together are
heavily outnumbered by the 72.3 per cent who made no change
in the status of their residential areas.

TABLE 5.15
Zone-to-zone mobility, by per capita *income*

Moved or stayed	% of all families in the sample	% of families with less than 1,000 forints per head	% of families with more than 1,000 forints per head
Remained in high status areas	26.9	22.0	30.0
Remained in low status areas	45.4	49.0	41.0
Moved from low to high status area	16.0	15.0	18.0
Moved from high status to low status area	11.7	14.0	11.0
Total %	100.0	100.0	100.0

Within the minority who did change their 'district status',
the figures show some net improvements for all classes, but
rather more of it for the higher classes. Among the higher
income group, 62 per cent of those who moved to zones of
different status moved 'upwards' and 38 per cent moved 'downwards'. Among the lower income group the proportions are
respectively 52 per cent and 48 per cent.

As old inhabitants moved, the housing they vacated was reoccupied, most often by new immigrants to the city. If the net upward movement of the old inhabitants signified some marginal desegregation, it was more than balanced by the greater segregation of the newcomers. This arose from the conjunction of the system of housing allocation with the social composition of the immigrant population. The data show that a fifth of all the blue-collar workers had moved directly from the country into their present urban housing, while only 5 or 6 per cent of white-collar workers had done so. At the same time a fifth of the white-collar workers had come from Budapest or other towns, while only 3 per cent of blue-collar workers had done so.

In other words, most white collar immigrants came from towns and most blue-collar immigrants came from the country. Looking now at the zones they came into, we find that 75 per cent of the rural immigrants live in zones of lower status while only 40 per cent of the urban immigrants do so. The immigrants are more sharply divided than the old inhabitants are, between high and low social strata: the proportions of intellectuals and unskilled blue-collar workers are higher among the immigrants, with lower proportions of clerical workers, technicians, and skilled workers from the middle strata.

It seems likely, therefore, that the pattern of zone-to-zone mobility within the cities combined with the biased social composition of the immigrants, and their tendency to go to particular zones, have tended to *increase rather than decrease the degree of social segregation in the cities as a whole*. Moreover, that increase of segregation did not arise simply from the market effects of people's individual preferences. It arose, to some extent at least, from the socialist policy of allocating land and housing by administrative rather than market methods.

CHAPTER 6
Ways of Life in Different Urban Zones

IN previous chapters the urban zones have been defined on the basis of their urban and economic functions, their location, and the composition of their housing stock. Zones defined on that basis prove to have distinctive social characteristics too, in the composition of their population. The processes of zone-to-zone migration—processes which are heavily influenced by state housing and planning policies—tend to increase rather than reduce the degree of social segregation from zone to zone.

The purpose of this chapter is to ask whether the social composition of the zones affects the living standards and conditions of their residents, and if so, to what extent. Theoretically this is a complex question. Our statistical indicators of 'way of life' are more closely correlated with social status (measured by education, occupation, and income) than with urban situation. We know that the various zones have different proportions of the social classes or status groups. So what we have to ask is this: are the differences in ways of life in the different zones *sufficiently* explained by the social status of the people in each zone—or are they *also* influenced by the status of those around them, for example by the degree and kind of social mixture or segregation of the zone? To put the question in another way, do families *of identical social status* fare differently if they live in zones *of different social composition?*

The data at our disposal do not provide a conclusive answer to the question. Nor indeed could any purely quantitative research do so. So, as a 'best guess', we will proceed on the hypothetical assumption that social status has *more* influence on way of life than urban situation does, but that they both have *some* influence.

Our findings do support some conclusions about the effects of planning policies on living conditions and residents' attitudes. The residents' attitudes are important not only as evidence about their experience, but also as a main element in the motivation of zone-to-zone migration. In what follows we look first at housing questions, then at other consumer behaviour.

Housing situation

The housing situation of the families who live in the different zones is determined partly by the quality of housing in the zones, partly by their urban services, and partly by their social composition. Previous chapters have discussed the physical qualities and equipment of the housing. We now look at some aspects of its size and social use.

TABLE 6.1

The size of housing units in the urban zones

Zone	% with 1 room	% with 2 rooms	% with 3 or more rooms	Number in sample
New multi-storey housing estates	11.4	76.6	12.0	122
City centre	34.4	42.6	23.0	550
Transitional zone I	25.0	49.4	25.6	188
Transitional zone II	44.5	39.2	16.3	360
Mixed industrial–residential areas	40.0	42.6	17.4	597
Outer suburbs of family houses	23.6	54.9	21.5	399

The size of the houses is not strongly correlated with the social status of the zones. It rather reflects the time when the houses were built. There are high proportions of one-roomed homes in the poorer transitional areas and the industrial–residential areas—but also in the city centre, which got many of its small flats after the Second World War, when the large *bourgeois* apartments were subdivided into smaller units. But very few new one-roomed flats have been built since then, so very few are to be found in the new housing estates or the outer suburbs. The predominance of two-roomed apartments in the new multi-storey estates reflects the unimaginative way they were designed for the phantom 'standard man' with 'standard family'—these most up-to-date areas actually have fewer three-roomed flats than do the deteriorating slums. The extreme physical homogeneity of the housing on the new estates has specially unfortunate effects. It tends to monotonize the estates both socially and intellectually. Three-generational families, families with many children, and families with any other non-standard characteristics tend to be excluded, by the lack of any housing adaptable to their needs. Of the families who do come, our data indicate that a needless proportion of the intellectuals soon depart again. They need studies to work in; the standard two-roomed flat does not allow a family to have children *and* a study, so many intellectuals move off to buy their own housing in the co-operative apartment-houses built by the state in the green-belt areas of the superior transitional zone.

In studying social effects of that kind we were not satisfied to use the occupation of the male head of the household as the only indicator of social status, as has been done in most of the analysis so far. We therefore constructed a composite index of family social status to represent husband's occupation, wife's occupation, and family income *per capita*. Into the highest stratum, for example, we put families in which both adults are intellectuals and income exceeds 1,000 forints per head of the family as a whole; into the lowest stratum we put families with an unskilled labourer as breadwinner and less than 800 forints of income per head. This is the basis of the social categories in the tables that follow.

The distribution of space and crowding of the social strata (Table 6.2) is rather more clear-cut than is the distribution of space and crowding of the urban zones (Table 6.3). Within and

TABLE 6.2

Social status, housing space and living density

Social status	Average number of rooms	Average number of people per room	Average area of home (square metres)
Upper	1.95	1.36	60.1
Upper middle	1.89	1.48	55.1
Middle	1.56	1.59	47.9
Lower middle	1.39	1.77	42.1
Lower	1.25	1.95	39.2

TABLE 6.3
People per room in the urban zones

Zone	% good: less than 1.5 per room	% reasonable: 1.5–2.0 per room	% bad: more than 2.0 per room	Number in sample
New multi-storey housing estates	42.2	40.1	17.4	192
City centre	39.5	36.4	24.1	546
Transitional zone I	43.1	37.2	19.7	188
Transitional zone II	37.7	30.4	31.9	358
Mixed industrial–residential areas	36.6	31.0	32.4	594
Outer suburbs of family houses	38.6	27.6	33.9	398

between urban zones the distribution of space is more complicated, partly because of the varying age of the housing. The average floor area of the apartments in the new multi-storey estates is not large; there are bigger houses in the city centre, and in the outer suburbs. The outer suburbs especially have comparatively low social status but their houses average about 70 square metres, and many of the new ones are 100 or more. All three of the zones with higher status than that have smaller-sized housing than that. To that extent, the advantages of size and status are spread around so that inequalities are not compounded. But they are compounded, as always, in the poorer transitional zone. There and in the industrial areas the houses and flats average about 40 square metres, and small housing also means poor housing. So the low status of the families, the houses, and the zones tend to be superimposed to put the residents at the greatest possible disadvantage.

Patterns of consumption

Spending patterns are of course constrained by family income. The average monthly *per capita* income is 1,300 forints in the new multi-storey estates, 1,100 forints in the city centre and the better transitional zone, and around 900 forints in the poorer transitional zone. That is income per head. Whole family monthly income ranges from about 3,700 forints in the multi-storey estates to about 2,400 forints in the poorer transitional zone. Those differences in spending power are not reduced by the service costs of the housing. Those monthly costs—for rent, heating, electricity, water, gas—are highest in the multi-storey estates and in the poorer transitional zone, in both of which they average about 500 forints. They are lowest, at about 280 forints, in the industrial–residential areas. In the outer suburbs they climb again to average 444 forints. But, as noticed earlier, the people do not generally perceive these inequities. Much the same number everywhere—about 20 per cent in each zone—think their housing costs excessive.

There are significant differences in spending on consumer durables. In the multi-storey estate the families had spent an average 21,000 forints on furniture through the previous five years. In the superior transitional zone and some of the outer suburban areas the average was 15,000 forints. In the city centre it was 10,000 forints. In the poorer transitional zone it was between 6,000 and 7,000 forints. In the multi-storey estates nearly a quarter of the families had spent more than 30,000 forints on furniture; in the poorer transitional zone only 1 per cent had spent as much as that. The high-income groups in the multi-storey estates can spend more on durables because they save more: family monthly savings on those estates average 300 forints, compared with 120–150 forints in the zones of lower status. In both cases the averages conceal wide differences between households. Forty-four per cent in the multi-storey estates say they cannot accumulate savings at all; about 60 per cent in the other zones say they cannot.

Expenditure is differently distributed for different household items. Refrigerators go with status: 79 per cent of households in the multi-storey estates have one, 37 per cent in the superior transitional zone, 30 per cent in the city centre, and only 10 per cent in the zones of lowest status. But washing machines and television sets appear to be classless. Sixty-eight per cent of all households own a washing machine, 64 per cent have television, and for those items there are no significant differences between zones.

It is harder to measure in any exact way what determines how intensively people use the goods and services available to them. Obviously people with more money to spend use more urban services. But is that usage affected by urban situation as

well as by income? In the course of our work we asked a great
many families whether they were in the habit of going out to
restaurants or coffee houses, whether they used public
laundries, whether they employed a housemaid. The answers
seemed to us to be determined by occupation and income, and
sometimes by the age or origin of the people concerned, rather
than by the zones in which they lived. There were still some
minor differences between zones. Some were dictated by the
accessibility of the services concerned. Others seemed rather to
have demographic causes. The poorer transitional areas tend to
have older households with more conservative habits; both tend
to be backward in making use of the more novel urban facilities.
The new multi-storey estates have the fullest array of services,
and young, urban-bred populations who are quick to use them.
Some similar differences, from similar causes, can be observed
in the cultural and recreational preferences of those who respectively go out a lot, and stay home a lot.

Satisfaction with housing and urban situation

We have noted that the quality of housing varies from social
class to social class, but that people's feelings about it do not
vary as widely as the actual quality of the housing does. Their
feelings about their housing situation vary rather more widely
from urban zone to urban zone.

The satisfaction of the people in the newly-built areas is
striking, and has very little relation to social class. Whether in
the favoured multi-storey estates or in the humbler outer

TABLE 6.4
Satisfaction with housing situation in the urban zones

Zone	% very satisfied	% satisfied	% dissatisfied	Number in sample
New multi-storey estates	81.2	8.9	9.9	192
City centre	50.7	21.7	27.6	548
Transitional zone I	57.0	23.2	19.8	190
Transitional zone II	44.2	27.2	28.6	380
Mixed industrial– residential areas	52.8	21.6	25.6	597
Outer suburbs of family houses	67.6	18.0	14.4	401

suburbs, most of the housing is new and the best of its kind; and, perhaps more important, it has been queued for or saved for or slaved for, or built with the residents' own hands, in ways that make it with special poignancy 'their own'. By contrast the highest dissatisfaction is experienced—also somewhat irrespective of social class—in the zones of old housing, whether capacious or mean. More than a quarter of the people in the city centre, the old industrial districts, and the poorer transitional zone are actively dissatisfied with their situations. The similar levels of satisfaction and dissatisfaction, despite substantial differences of housing cost and quality, indicate once again the realism with which the different social strata assess their chances, and set their expectations. Compare, for example, the critical spirit and impatient expectations of the intellectuals in the city centre with the modesty, and sometimes hopelessness, of the older and less skilled blue-collar workers in the older zones of lower status. It is true that the poorest zones have the highest percentages of dissatisfied residents. But first, the differences in dissatisfaction are not nearly as extensive as the real differences of situation. And second, as further evidence of the same modest realism, the proportions who intend or expect to move do not reflect the proportions who are dissatisfied (Table 6.5).

TABLE 6.5
Would-be mobility in the urban zones

Zone	% with no plans to move	% who plan to move within 2 or 3 years	% who hope to move some time	Number in sample
New housing estates	79.1	16.7	4.2	101
City centre	68.5	18.5	13.0	540
Transitional zone I	81.6	8.0	10.4	100
Transitional zone II	77.7	13.1	9.2	358
Mixed industrial–residential areas	75.3	15.0	9.7	504
Outer suburbs of family houses	82.6	10.4	7.0	402

Compare the poorer transitional zone with the multi-storey estates: the same small proportion expect to move, even though three times as many are positively dissatisfied. Except in the city centre, the proportions expecting to stay put are much the same in all zones. We conclude that people expect to move only if they know they *can* move, i.e. if they have some capital or saving capacity, or a house of some value to exchange, or some practical hope of state-rental housing. Those without the means do not develop the expectations. Many of those in that situation seem to go further, and begin to believe their present situation is better than it really is.

Of the families who want to move house, about half have reasons (to do with work, education, etc.) which are nothing to do with the housing itself. But half want to move because they are dissatisfied with their housing conditions. Included in that latter half are a fifth who want to escape from subletting arrangements so as to have homes entirely their own. A tenth want to move because their present housing is likely to be demolished. Those are city averages, but with one exception the proportions do not vary much from zone to zone. The exception is the new multi-storey estates. Though their apartments are larger than average, a higher proportion want to move because —as intellectuals of high status—they find the standard two-roomed apartments too small. Rooms tend to be larger in the superior transitional zone, especially in the new co-operative apartments; residents of those blocks who want to move are mostly young people sharing or subletting or living with parents—it is the sharing rather than the size of apartments that prompts them to go.

Dissatisfaction with their neighbourhoods is widespread among movers, but that alone does not seem to motivate people to move. On the other hand, those who want to move because of specific housing needs or dissatisfactions often add that they would also like a change of neighbourhood, and of the life-style that goes with the neighbourhood (Table 6.6).

People in the newly built zones—in the multi-storey estates, and in the family houses of the outer suburbs—tend to like the life-style which goes with the kind of housing they already have. So, of course, do many of the larger numbers in all zones who express no desire to move. Of those who would like to move from other zones, a third would like multi-storey apartments. (Some of these may be thinking of the financial advantages rather than the life-style of the multi-storey estates. But that

TABLE 6.6
Types of housing into which people from urban zones would like to move

Zone	% who want old housing of several storeys	% who want new multi-storey apartment housing	% who want apartment housing of 1–3 storeys	% who want family house and garden	% not sure	Number in sample
New multi-storey housing estates	2.6	68.4	10.5	15.6	2.9	38
City centre	9.3	33.2	16.3	26.7	14.5	172
Transitional zone I	2.9	31.4	17.1	40.0	8.6	35
Transitional zone II	3.7	38.1	7.3	34.9	16.0	80
Mixed industrial–residential areas	4.1	33.3	6.8	44.9	10.9	147
Outer suburbs of family houses	1.4	26.6	4.2	56.4	11.4	71

factor is less likely to have distorted the other preferences, because of the lesser financial advantages of the other types of housing.) A more interesting conclusion, because it contradicts the conventional wisdom of the experts, is that, if the housing preferences of the 'movers' (see Table 6.6) do express the preferences of those who for the time being are not contemplating a move, then one might expect that about half the families in the two cities are attracted by family houses and the suburban life-style that goes with them. To that number we should probably add those who opt for the new, small co-operative apartment houses, because those also offer access to private gardens and other features of suburban life. That takes the suburban preference to about 60 per cent, leaving only 40 per cent who desire the more urbanized life-style of the city centre and the multi-storey estates.

However, if we probe further into this pattern of responses, we strike a paradox which may perhaps conceal an important early warning to policy-makers. The figures in Table 6.6 come from responses to questions about people's satisfaction with their present housing, and about intentions to move. They can probably be taken as 'realist' answers. But, if a similar question is asked in a context which invites 'ideal' answers, and if it is asked of all the respondents rather than merely the minority who intend to move house, then the overall response is different and also differs from city to city. The different responses from Pecs and Szeged may be illuminating if we want to learn more about the motivation of these urban attitudes, so the two are separated in Table 6.7. People were asked to assess and compare the urban zones in a general way, and to say which zone they would ideally prefer to live in.

TABLE 6.7

Urban zones thought most attractive and desirable to live in in Pecs and Szeged

Zone	% who think it the most attractive zone		% who would ideally like to live there	
	Szeged	Pecs	Szeged	Pecs
New housing estates	13.9	31.9	9.6	34.3
City centre	56.9	17.8	50.5	25.2
Transitional zone I	10.8	37.6	11.2	18.2
Total of all higher status zones	81.6	87.3	71.3	77.7
Total of all lower status zones	18.4	12.7	28.7	22.3

Eighty or ninety per cent of the families in both cities think the higher status zones are the most attractive, and nearly as many would like to live in one of them. That means that 80 per cent of the population would like to live in zones that actually accommodate only 40 per cent of them. The preference runs through all classes, from 90 per cent of high bureaucrats and intellectuals to 60 per cent, which is still an absolute majority, of blue-collar workers. Among the favoured zones, the intellectuals would prefer the city centre or the co-operative apartment-houses of the green belt. The multi-storey estates are their last preference, 'ideally', but many nevertheless have to go there as the only way to get modern, fully-serviced housing. We observe that, if the city centre and the transitional zones were to be reconstructed in the 'organic' manner of sensitive urban renewal, so that they came to include a wide variety of housing choices, including options of good modern housing, then the intelligentsia would rush to those areas, and the multi-storey estates would rapidly deteriorate. It is not fanciful to fear that one by-product of generally better housing and planning policies might thus be to turn what are now élite estates into out-of-town slums. That is the more likely because 40 per cent of the blue-collar families who want to move would like to move into those multi-storey estates. (They do not feel constrained to go there, as some intellectuals do; they are positively attracted by better conditions than they have at present.) Under present policies most workers will not get into those estates, they will perforce build family houses. But they do not *prefer* family houses to any greater extent than other occupational groups do. Thirty four per cent of the unskilled workers would prefer family houses—but so would 38 per cent of the high bureaucrats. Their motives may differ—the worker's family may be leaving one room and a kitchen due for demolition for the better facilities of a family house, while the bureaucrat's family may be leaving the excellent facilities of a multi-storey apartment to get more rooms and more space in a family house. But, whatever their purposes, we have seen that their chances of getting what they want differ a great deal. Bureaucrats and intellectuals who want family houses do not have serious difficulty in getting them. But workers who want multi-storey apartments are quite unlikely to get them. Forty per cent of the heads of households in both cities are unskilled; 34 per cent of the unskilled would like multi-storey apartments; only 3 per cent have got them. It is class discrimination by the state, rather than their own preference, that keeps the workers out of the privileged estates.

More than three-quarters of the families think the higher status zones the most attractive. Only 40 per cent live there. But three-quarters of them have no intention of moving, so we cannot conclude that many are too dissatisfied with the districts in which they live.

Besides being realistic about their housing chances, the families are also realistic about the objective characteristics of the urban zones (Tables 6.8, 6.9, 6.10, 6.11, 6.12, and 6.13).

Tables 6.9 to 6.13 are printed one after another in order to illustrate a human paradox. The first five tables report the people's objective assessment of the concrete characteristics of their zones. Averaging the responses to the first four questions, we could say that 54.7 per cent of the people living in the city centre, 46.8 per cent in the multi-storey estates, 32.0 per cent in the better transitional zone, 17.2 per cent in the outer suburbs, 17.2 per cent in the poorer transitional zone, and 12.4 per cent in the industrial–residential areas are satisfied with their zones. We could also say that the assessments were objective, and

TABLE 6.8
Residents's assessment of the public utilities in their urban zones

Zone	% who think services better than average	% who think services average	% who think services worse than average	Number in sample
New multi-storey estates	64.9	25.4	9.7	134
City centre	54.8	35.7	9.5	356
Transitional zone I	28.4	58.1	13.5	141
Transitional zone II	12.9	43.7	43.4	240
Mixed industrial–residential areas	7.5	42.5	50.0	388
Outer suburbs of family houses	8.8	39.1	52.1	274

TABLE 6.9
Residents' assessment of transport services in their urban zones

Zone	% who think transport better than average	% who think transport average	% who think transport worse than average	Number in sample
New multi-storey estates	38.1	30.6	31.3	134
City centre	63.2	30.1	6.7	356
Transitional zone I	38.3	52.5	9.2	141
Transitional zone II	34.0	43.6	22.4	241
Mixed industrial–residential areas	23.1	51.8	25.1	390
Outer suburbs of family houses	16.4	55.2	28.4	275

TABLE 6.10
Residents' assessment of commercial shops and services in their urban zones

Zone	% who think shops etc. above average	% who think shops etc. average	% who think shops etc. below average	Number in sample
New multi-storey estates	19.4	45.5	35.1	134
City centre	56.9	36.1	7.0	375
Transitional zone I	24.1	61.0	14.9	141
Transitional zone II	14.9	59.9	25.2	242
Mixed industrial–residential areas	9.5	65.1	25.4	390
Outer suburbs of family houses	7.6	53.5	38.9	275

TABLE 6.11
Residents's assessment of the attractiveness of their urban zones

Zone	% who think it one of the most attractive	% who think it average	% who think it ugly	Number in sample
New multi-storey estates	54.5	40.3	5.2	134
City centre	43.8	47.5	8.7	356
Transitional zone I	36.9	54.6	8.5	141
Transitional zone II	11.6	63.2	25.2	242
Mixed industrial–residential area	9.5	56.5	34.0	388
Outer suburbs of family houses	37.5	53.3	9.2	272

TABLE 6.12
The least-liked zones in the two cities

Zone most disliked	% of Szeged respondents	% of Pecs respondents
Mixed industrial–residential areas	49.8	60.0
Transitional zone II	38.9	14.3
Outer suburbs of family houses	9.4	13.3
New multi-storey estates	1.2	10.5
Transitional zone I	0.4	1.3
City centre	0.3	0.6

TABLE 6.13
Residents' general attitudes to their own zones in the two cities

Attitudes to own zone	% in Szeged	% in Pecs	% in both cities
Like it very much	72.2	71.2	72.6
Like it	15.1	16.6	15.9
Indifferent to it	7.1	4.5	4.8
Dislike it	5.6	7.7	6.7

agreed with the actual distribution of the various services to the zones. And yet, when the same people are asked whether or not they like living in their own zones, 90 per cent answered 'yes'!

We cannot offer much in the way of psychological or social explanation of this paradox. We can merely report that we have come across it wherever we have asked such questions in the course of our research. As citizens, an overall satisfaction—a kind of psychological identification—with our situation seems to be produced quite independently of the more obvious facts of the situation. Thus we are capable of declaring something to be wrong in many particular aspects, but right (or anyway satisfying) as a whole. In the Hungarian cities, the more concrete our questions the more critical the answers were; the more general the questions, the more satisfied or positively 'attached to the place' the people would say they were. We drew the methodological conclusion that research into public satisfaction should generally use concrete questions. There are simple psychological reasons why most people, most of the time, give 'satisfied' answers to questions of any vague or general kind. People who have managed to move need to believe they were not mistaken, so they approve of their new situation. People who have lived long in the same situation cannot easily say they are dissatisifed with it, because that is to admit that they are dissatisfied with the life they have spent there. If people in an ugly or inconvenient situation have been unable to move, a true assessment of the situation may seem to imply a confession of failure; so they may tell others, and perhaps themselves, that the situation is not really so bad, after all. What this demonstrates is the adaptability of human nature and its capacity to suffer disadvantage cheerfully. Such modest or defensive patience in adversity should not be cited by urbanistic experts to justify inequitable planning policies. We should always treat with critical anxiety the obejctive inequalities in urban society, and the mechanisms which produce them and maintain them.

Conclusions

1. We divide the cities into six zones on the basis of their historical formation, their housing, and their economic and urban functions. The zones are: the city centre; a superior transitional zone in and around the greenbelt; a deteriorating transitional zone; mixed industrial–residential areas; outer suburbs of family housing; and new multi-storey housing estates. In their infrastructural provisions the city

centre, the superior transitional zone, and the new multi-storey estates are generally superior, the other zones generally inferior. The superior zones house 40 per cent of the population, the inferior zones 60 per cent. The superior occupational groups—bureaucrats, intellectuals, clerical workers, technicians, and people retired from those occupations—tend to live in the superior zones. Blue-collar workers tend to live in the inferior zones. To be more precise, in the superior zones 70 per cent of the people are of superior status; in the inferior zones 70 per cent of the people are of inferior status. That measures the degree of segregation in the urban society.

2. Movement between the zones is not, on balance, reducing their segregation. The continuing improvement of housing and urban services may moderate the internal segregational process a little in the long run. But that effect is counterbalanced by the way the cities receive immigrants. Most incoming intellectual and white-collar workers come into the city centre or the new multi-storey estates. Rural immigrants, and blue-collar workers from other cities, move into the low status zones. So the process of urban growth constantly reinforces the segregation.

3. Housing policy, credit policy, and urban planning policy all intensify the segregational process in one way or another. Housing administration does so by concentrating the 'administered' housing stock in a few zones and allocating most of it to intellectual and other white-collar groups and a few of the most skilled blue-collar workers. A similar favouritism governs the allocation of credit, and of the high-quality housing which public agencies build for sale. Credit to buy apartments in new co-operative apartment buildings will go to families with higher incomes. Planning policy enforces segregation in a number of ways. It concentrates most state housing development in exclusive areas. It reserves the best new urban zones for the kinds of large-scale construction which only the state building enterprises can do. It does not allow much individual rehabilitation or replacement of housing in the deteriorating transitional and industrial zones. And it confines the biggest single class of homeseeker—the worker who wants to build for himself—to the outer suburbs, because independent small-scale build-

ing is permitted scarcely anywhere else. These policies have direct effects in segregating the social classes from one another, and also indirect effects through the patterns of mobility which they encourage. In the old, deteriorating zones, ambitious families are not allowed to build or re-build better housing for themselves, so they depart as soon as they can, usually to the outer suburbs, and their old accommodation is typically taken by the least successful of the unskilled blue-collar immigrants to the city. Thus the old areas become more homogeneous and disadvantaged than ever. Although the outer suburbs are as heavily segregated as the transitional areas, their situation cannot be said to be critical: they have generally good and up-to-date housing, occupied by energetic young working-class families who are satisfied with many aspects of their housing situation. It is in the poorer transitional zones and the older, poorer parts of the industrial districts that physical and social and demographic influences converge to generate slums and ensure that they continue to deteriorate, socially as well as physically. These are the most critical areas of Hungary's cities, and they are in urgent need of extensive reconstruction.

CHAPTER 7

Socialist Planning and Urban Ecological Change in Eastern Europe

THE foregoing analysis suggests that the socio-ecological structure of the two sample cities is changing. There are theoretical and empirical grounds for believing that similar changes are in process in many other cities in Hungary, and more generally in Eastern Europe. A main purpose of this book is to show that this pattern of change in Eastern Europe is a unique one. The socialist cities are moving away from the patterns characteristic of West European and North American cities. While it is true that the particular pattern of any city's development can only be fully explained by its particular situation and history, we nevertheless believe that some common causes are working to produce some common urban effects through most of Eastern Europe, and we offer the hypothesis that the emerging pattern is a new one which can only be understood and explained as a product of particular types of socialist economic and urban planning.

It can be no more than a tentative hypothesis because at the time of our studies there had been so little systematic research into the ecology of the cities concerned. In the 1960s there were Czech studies of Ostrava, similar to our studies of Pecs and Szeged, under the direction of J. Musil. For their results, see Zdenek Rysavy (1969). Other works by Musil, and by Z. Pioro in Poland, were also accessible. So were some earlier studies by the present authors, which suggested that the patterns revealed in Pecs and Szeged were even clearer in Budapest and some other Hungarian cities. It is from such patchy sources, plus general knowledge of the history of the area, that we must now draw together our conclusions.

For ten years or so after the Second World War, resources were concentrated on repairing the damage done (and the maintenance neglected) through the war years. There was not yet much sign of distinctively socialist policy in the physical development of the cities. Except in cities such as Warsaw which had been completely destroyed and had to be completely rebuilt, the first decade of socialist work tended to restore and reconstruct the cities' traditional forms.

It is from the middle 1950s that Eastern urban policies diverge decisively from Western urban models. At that time the urban planners got access to larger (though still modest) resources, and began the deliberate reconstruction of the cities. They also began the unequal allocation of resources to the various urban zones, which explains the increasing differentiation of the zones from that date to this.

In Hungary since 1956 there has been reasonably steady investment in city centres. Their roads and services have been improved. Business and administrative activity have expanded, mostly into new institutional buildings of generally high quality. These have displaced and reduced the residential uses of city centres, but not as completely as in (for example) most American central business districts—some good quality housing survives in the Hungarian centres, in a few new buildings, and in many old ones modernized. Although the extent of central investment and reconstruction varies from city to city, there have been significant amounts in all cities.

The next focus of developmental investment, in both infrastructure and buildings, is the new multi-storey housing estate. In almost all East European cities, state-owned housing development is mostly concentrated in large homogeneous estates. Those estates get the best new housing and (however delayed even the best may sometimes be) the best new urban services. (The reasons for their particular forms and privileges were discussed in our book *The Sociological Problems of the New Housing Estates*, 1969, pp. 16–18.)

Between the city centre and some privileged extensions of it which we have called the first or superior transitional zone, and the new housing estates at the urban outskirts, there has been very little urban development of any kind for half a century. What we have called the second or poorer transitional zone and the industrial–residential zone have both deteriorated, and in recent decades planning and housing policies have forced them to deteriorate faster. The new authorities believe these areas should eventually be replaced by comprehensive redevelopment, including comprehensive replacement of the old street patterns and services; i.e. in Western language they belong to the 'bulldozer' school of urban redevelopment. Comprehensive clearance and replacement would take such massive resources that there is no practical prospect of doing it for decades to come. Nevertheless, that is the official future of these zones, so for the time being the authorities forbid any piecemeal reconstruction or replacement of their fabric. In many areas, householders are not even allowed to do routine repair and maintenance to their houses. So public policy condemns these zones to deteriorate faster than ever, under what Western planners call 'planning blight'.

The outer suburbs attract a good deal of private investment, in the form of new family houses for working-class families. These suburbs need public investment in roads and urban services. They rarely get it very fully or punctually, though this varies from country to country. In Hungary the city authorities provide the outer-suburban subdivisions, and eventually service them. In Poland (at the time of our study) urban planning regulations prohibited the building of new family houses, so they had to be built outside the cities' administrative boundaries, where they had to rely entirely on local municipalities for any development of roads, services, and other infrastructure.

Taken together, the zones and their shares of public investment can be depicted as shown in Figure 7.1. The zones as indicated are categorized, rather than mapped geographically. The cities do not in fact grow in concentric circles, and it is not our aim to explain their growth in strictly geographical terms. But the symbolic circles are not entirely inappropriate: distance from the centre has a good deal to do with the age and social composition of the zones. With that qualification, the above sketch dramatizes a socialist urban planning version of what Jane Jacobs, in *The Death and Life of Great American Cities* (1961), called 'cataclysmic' urban planning. She used the word to characterize policies which deprive most areas of investment most of the time, in order to concentrate investment into particular areas for particular short periods. She argued that such action tended to be doubly destructive: it did drastic harm where the sudden investment did occur, and ensured steady deterioration where it did not. Sane urban investment, by contrast, should be more evenly distributed over space and time

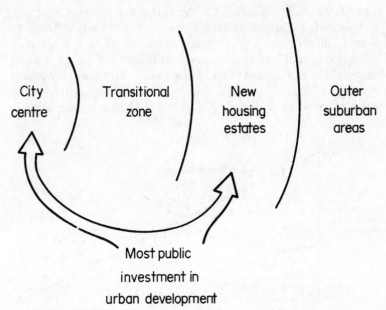

| City centre | Transitional zone | New housing estates | Outer suburban areas |

Most public
investment in
urban development

FIG. 7.1   Zones and their shares of public investment

to allow all areas of the city to adapt and change organically all the time.

The new policies are transforming the socialist cities. Traditionally, the East European cities were similar in ecological structure to those of Western Europe: the social status of the population tended to be highest at the city centre, and declined gradually towards the outskirts, where it was lowest. This pattern was never universal—English cities differed from it, and North American cities often reversed it altogether with status rising from central slums to arcadian outer suburbs. What Eastern Europe seems to be creating now is yet another structure. It is not the old European pattern, it is not the North American pattern, and it is not a passing phase in a transition from one of those to the other. It is of a new kind, and we tentatively characterize it as follows:

The social status of the city centre declines somewhat, chiefly because of its declining residential numbers. The social status of the transitional zones declines rather faster. There is then high status in the new housing estates, but low status again in the rest of the outer suburbs. Of the two zones of low status, the deteriorating transitional zones are not yet entirely reduced to slums, so that the lowest social status of all is in the outer suburbs, even if physical housing conditions and 'housing satisfaction' are not so bad there. Simplifying extremely, the North American, East European, and West European patterns may be compared as shown in Figure 7.2. Of course those simpli-

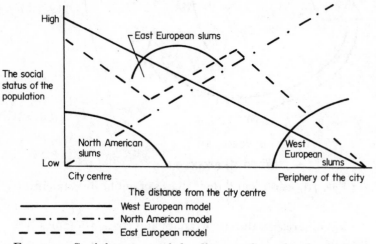

FIG. 7.2   Social status and the distance from the city centre

fications are excessive. For example, West European cities are not all of one pattern. Some have patches of slum or low status near their centres. In France and West Germany there is significant 'suburbanization' of the North American kind, though Italian cities seem so far to be quite immune to it. To some extent, where the land and the old fabric allow it, suburbanization responds to the rise of car ownership: before the motor car, North American cities had much closer resemblance to the European model. But, even if Western Europe is beginning a transition to something more like the North American model, our theme here is that Eastern Europe is not. It is developing a third model, all its own. In this model the deteriorating zones are situated in different parts of the city, the causes of their deterioration are different, the zones of high status are in different parts of the city, and their ecological character is different. Compared with most North American cities, the segregation of the East European cities is more moderate—as also are most of their urban and social inequalities.

The hypothesis of a new, third model of urban development cannot be defined precisely, nor can it be verified in any conclusive way by the evidence available so far. Much more elaborate research would be required. But it is obvious that the mode of production that has been characteristic of early socialism has had profound effects on the ecology of the East European cities. The changed pattern of ownership, especially of land, has had important effects. So has the new distribution of income. So has the new role of the state in housing and urban planning. Some of the effects of the new public policies may be very different from the planners' intentions, but they are fairly direct: East European planners do not rely very much on indirect methods of management and motivation, such as regulation and taxation, because they assume they have unlimited powers of direct intervention through their programmes of public investment and housing allocation.

Besides its theoretical interest, a better understanding of the new urban processes may be important for planning praxis. The planners and managers of urban development must come to terms with the fact that the city is *a system*. Any one intervention in the system is likely to have more than one effect. If the direct, intended effect of the intervention is good, it does not follow that the indirect and second round effects must all be good too. A new housing estate in one area may hasten the growth of a slum somewhere else. An architectural design policy for one area may have powerful social and economic effects on the life of that and other areas. Especially in housing, architectural uniformity will often be the enemy of social equality: new estates or districts of homogeneous architectural design will almost invariably increase the social segregation and inequality of the city as a whole.

These considerations are especially important in the evaluation of strategies for urban reform and reconstruction. In cities like those which have been the subjects of this study, it is clear that increasing segregation, inequality, and physical deterioration of the old transitional and industrial zones can only be averted if the state ceases to concentrate urban investment on the construction and infrastructure of new housing estates. Resources need to be switched to the reconstruction of the transitional zones. That may sound banal, since it is safe to say that all urban planners and bureaucrats in all East European cities have been battling for some decades to get the resources necessary to increase the rate of demolition and redevelopment of precisely those zones. They have generally lost to the industrial investors, who continue to pre-empt a lion's share of the available capital funds. But our analysis suggests that their preferred approach would be as counter-effective as their investments in the multi-storey estates have been, in reducing segregation or improving urban equalities. With scarcely any exceptions they believe their role is to demolish and replace the transitional zones, by comprehensive bulldozing methods. That intention is written into all their Master Plans. They justify it by reference to fashionable theories of design and development which offer no prospect of improvement until the old road patterns are removed and replaced; and they justify it by claiming that it would cost as much to rehabilitate and maintain the old fabric as to demolish and replace it. In short, they offer the case for comprehensive redevelopment which has been widely discredited in the West (see, for example, Anderson, 1964) and they reinforce it with additional arguments for the 'socialist uniformities' which comprehensive redesign is expected to make possible.

As sociologists our first interest is in the likely social consequences of such a process. First, it necessarily destroys a certain amount of good housing along with the bad, so it promises some overall loss of housing value. Second, the proposal is to extend the new housing estates inwards towards the city centre, by building more dense multi-storey state housing on the sites cleared by the bulldozer. Such developments would have the housing class composition of the existing multi-storey estates, and (like those estates) their housing would be allocated to a social class of similar homogeneity—mostly young families with high status and income. The new housing would not be available to the people displaced from the old housing that was demolished. On the contrary, it would be both the newest and the best-placed, most central housing available, so it would transform the rebuilt areas from the poorest to the richest, most élite districts of the city.

Meanwhile the preliminary demolitions would have two effects. They would evict large numbers of families of low income and status without offering them any alternative housing in the same zones; and they would absolutely reduce the amount of modest low-priced housing available in the inner urban areas. More demand and less supply would raise the price of whatever deteriorating old housing remained, at the expense of the classes least able to pay. So a reconstruction which aims at the destruction and replacement of the segregated slums is likely, instead, to move them from place to place and actually increase their segregation, and the cumulative disadvantages of their people.

Instead of that self-defeating programme, our analysis suggests a more organic strategy of urban development. The reconstruction of the deteriorating zones should be designed to achieve an increasing mixture of housing classes and consequently of social classes. That could be achieved partly by differentiating new construction to include diverse types of housing to attract diverse groups of people, and partly by mixing the new housing with a good deal of the existing old housing, preserved and modernized as necessary, but continuing to house its old inhabitants, or successors like them.

In considering a more mixed, selective, organic mode of urban renewal we should not be too impressed by contrary economic arguments. In the first place, they may be dubious on their own grounds—wherever comprehensive redevelopment has been done it has proved to be more destructive and expensive than expected. In the second place, the net economic gain or loss is not the only relevant consideration—questions of economic equality and social integration may be at least as important. In the third place, the conservation and rehabilitation of old housing need not always be as expensive as the East European planners and economists fear. Indeed, expensive reconstruction to bring the old housing up to the standards of currently-built new housing could often defeat the purposes of conservation, by transferring the housing to an altogether different social class. A more modest planning aim would often be more acceptable: some new housing of varying type and quality should be patched into the old areas to attract diverse types of people into them; and a good deal of their older housing should be modestly improved without disturbing or displacing the people living in it.

If some urban planners object that such modest improvements would still cost nearly as much as new housing, the sociologist can only repeat the question which has been asked already so many times in this book: 'Too expensive *for whom?*' The capital invested in rehabilitating old houses will improve the houses of one class or group of people. If it were invested instead in demolishing and replacing those houses, its benefits would go to quite different people. Behind the seemingly abstract economic, technical, or urbanistic debates on housing or urban planning policies, the clash of social interests is revealed.

References

Anderson, Martin: *The Federal Bulldozer*, Cambridge, Massachusetts Institute of Technology Press, 1964.

Andorka, Rudolf: *A társadalmi átrétegződés és demográfiai hatásai Magyarországon. A Népességtudományi Kutató Intézet Kozleményei 30*, Budapest, 1970.

Baranov, A. V.: 'O sotzialnoy modely zilishsta', *Stroyitelstvo i Architectura*, 1969, No. 10.

Barbolet, R. H.: *Housing Classes and the Socio-ecological System*, London, Centre for Environmental Studies, 1969.

Burns, Leland, Thompson, Cecil, and Tjios, Khing: *Report on Pilot Study of Worker Productivity in Relation to Housing Conditions*, Los Angeles, Real Estate Research Program, Graduate School of Business Administration, University of California, 1965.

Castells, Manuel: 'La Fin de la sociologie urbaine', *Sociologie et Société*, 1969, No. 2.

Castells, Manuel: *The Urban Question*, first published 1972, Arnold, 1977.

Chombart de Lauwe, Paul: *Famille et habitation*, Vols. I–II, Paris, Centre National de la Recherche Scientifique, 1959–60.

Don, Martindale: 'Prefatory Remarks, the Theory of the City', in Max Weber: *The City*, New York, The Free Press, 1958.

Duric, Vojislav: 'Stanovanijc kao drustvena pojava i kao predmet sociologih izucavanja', *Sociológija*, 1969, No. 3, pp. 417–40.

Ferge, Zsuzsa: *Társadalmunk rétegződése*, Budapest, Közgazdasági és Jogi Könyvkiadó, 1969.

Festinger, Leo *et al.*: *Social Pressure in Informal Groups—a Study of Human Factors in Housing*, New York, Harper and Row, 1950.

Fischer, E. M. and Winnick, L. B.: 'A reformulation of the Filtering Concept', *Journal of Social Issues*, 1951, No. 1–2, pp. 47–85.

Gans, Herbert: 'The Human Implications of Slum Clearance and Relocation' *Journal of the American Institute of Planners*, 1959, February, pp. 15–29.

Gans, Herbert: 'Planning and Social Life', *Journal of the American Institute of Planners*, 1961, May, pp. 134–40.

Gans, Herbert: 'The Balanced Community. Homogeneity or Heterogeneity in Residential Areas?' *Journal of the American Institute of Planners*, 1961, August, pp. 176–84.

154   *Urban Social Inequalities*

Gans, Herbert: 'The Failure of Urban Renewal: A Critique and some Proposals', *Commentary*, 1965, April, pp. 29–37.

Glass, Ruth: 'Urban Sociology' in *Society: Problems and Methods of Study* (ed. A. T. Welford, M. Argyle, D. V. Glass, and J. N. Morris), London, Routledge and Kegan Paul, 1962, pp. 481–97.

Gliszczynski, Franciszek: 'Problematyka przestrzenna sytuacji mieszkaniowej i budownictwa mieszkaniowego Warszawy i jej strefy podmiejskiej', *Studia Komitet Przestrazennego Zagospodarowania Kraju*, Polskiej Akademii Nauk-Tom, XXI, Warszawa, 1967.

Greer, Scott: *Urban Renewal and American Cities*, Indianapolis, Bobbs-Merrill, 1965.

Greer, Scott: 'Problems of Housing and the Renewal of the City', in H. S. Becker (ed.): *Social Problems*, New York, John Wiley and Sons, 1966, pp. 517–48.

Grigsby, W. G.: *Housing Markets and Public Policy* (Philadelphia: University of Pennsylvania Press, 1963), especially the chapter on 'Filtering Process', pp. 84–110.

Hegedüs, András, and Márkus, Mária: 'Alternativa és értékválasztás az elosztás és fogyasztás távlati tervezésében', *Közgazdasági Szemle*, 1969, No. 9, pp. 1048–61.

Jacobs, Jane: *The Death and Life of Great American Cities*, New York, Random House, 1961.

Konrád, G. and Szelényi, J.: 'A lakáselosztás szociológiai kérdései', *Valoság*, 1969, No. 9.

Liska, Tibor: 'A bérlakás-kereskedelem koncepciója', *Valóság*, 1969, No. 1, pp. 22–35.

Loring, William: 'Housing Characteristics and Social Disorganization', *Journal of Social Problems*, 1956, January, pp. 160–8.

Macková, Libuse: *Byty a obyvatele v typové vystavbe TO-6B a TO-8B*, Praha, Vyzkumny Ustav Vystavby a Architektury, 1970.

Macková, Libuse: *Vyoy domacnosti ve statni a druzstevni vystavbe*, Praha, Vyzkumny Ustav Vystavby a Architektury, 1971.

Maisel, S. and Winnick, L. B.: 'Family Housing Expenditures Elusive Law and Intrusive Variances', in W. Wheaton *et al.* (ed.): *Urban Housing*, New York, The Free Press, 1966, pp. 139–53.

Merton, R. K.: 'The Social Psychology of Housing', in W. Dennis (ed.): *Current Trends in Social Psychology*, Pittsburg, University of Pittsburg Press, 1948, pp. 163–88.

Merton, R. K. *et al.*: *Patterns of Social Life, Explorations in the Sociology and Social Psychology of Housing*, New York, Bureau of Applied Social Research, 1950.

Meyerson, M. *et al.* (ed.): 'Housing and the National Economy' in *Housing, People and Cities*, New York, McGraw-Hill, 1962, pp. 19–31.

Miller, S. M. and Rein, M.: 'Poverty, Inequality and Policy', in H. S. Becker (ed.): *Social Problems*, New York, John Wiley and Sons, 1966, pp. 426–516.

Mitchell, R. E.: 'Some Social Implications of High Density Housing', *American Sociological Review*, 1971, February, pp. 18–29.

Mód, Aladárné, Ferge, Zsuzsa, Láng, Györgyné, and Kemény, István: *Társadalmi rétegződés Magyarországon. Statisztikai Időszaki Közlemények 90*, Budapest, 1966.

Musil, Jiri: 'Sociology of Urban Redevelopment Areas. A Study from Czechoslovakia', unpublished manuscript, n.d.

Musil, Jiri: 'The Development of Prague's Ecological Structure', in R. Pahl: *Readings in Urban Sociology*, London, Pergamon Press, 1968, pp. 232–59.

Musil, Jiri: 'Town Planning as a Social Process', *New Atlantis*, 1970, No. 2.

Pahl, R.: *Spatial Structure and Social Structure*, London, Centre for Environmental Studies, 1968.

Pahl, R.: *Urban Social Theory and Research—Environment and Planning*, 1969, pp. 143–53.

Pahl, R.: *Patterns of Urban Life*, London, Longmans, Green, 1970.

Pahl, R.: 'Collective Consumption and the State in Capitalist and State Socialist Societies', in Scase, R. (ed.): *Cleavage and Constraint*, London, Allen and Unwin, 1977.

Pap, Mária, and Pléh, Csaba: 'Általános iskolás gyermekek nyelvhasználata Budapesten', *Szociológia*, 1972, No. 2.

Pioró, Zygmunt: 'Niektóre czynniki ksztaltujace struktury i procesy ekologiczne wspolczesnych miast polskich', in S. Nowakowski: *Socjologiczne problemy miasta polskiego*, Warszawa, Panstwowe Wydawnictwo Naukowe, 1964, pp. 211–39,

Polanyi, K.: 'The Economy as Instituted Process', in K. Polanyi *et al.* (eds): *Trade and Market in Early Empires*, New York, The Free Press, 1957, pp. 12–20.

Rainwater, L.: 'A Decent Standard of Living: From Subsistence to Membership', Paper presented at the XIth International Family Research Seminar, London, 1970.

Ratcliff, R. U.: 'Filtering Down and the Elimination of Sub-standard Housing', *Journal of Land and Public Utility Economics*, 1945, November, pp. 322–30.

Ratcliff, R. U.: *Urban Land Economics*, New York, McGraw-Hill, 1949.

Rex, J. A.: 'The Sociology of a Zone of Transition', in R. Pahl (ed.): *Reading in Urban Sociology*, London, Pergamon Press, 1968, pp. 211–31.

Riemer, S.: 'Architecture for Family Living', *Journal of Social Issues*, 1951, No. 1–2, pp. 140–51.

Rocznik Statysticzny, 1970.

Rossi, P.: *Why Families Move*, New York, The Free Press, 1956.

Rysavy, Zdenek: 'Die gegenwärtige sozial-ökologische Struktur der Industriestadt Ostrau', in *Sozialempirische Materialien zur Stadtsoziologie*, Karlsruhe, Institut für Wirtschafts und Sozialwissenschaften der Universität Karlsruhe, 1969.

Slomczynski, Kazimierz M., and Wesolowski, Wlodzimierz: 'Zroznicowanie spoleczne: podstawowe wyniki', in W. Weselowski (ed.), *Zroznicowanie spoleczne*, Warszawa, Ossolineum, 1970, pp. 93–146.

Szelényi, Iván, and Konrád, György: *Az uj lakótelepek szociológiai problémái*, Budapest, Akadémiai Kiadó, 1969.

Szovosz, ___: Adatgyujtemeny a magyarorszagi lakashelyzet alakulasarol, Budapest, SZOVOSZ, 1969.

Vecernik, Jiri: 'Urbanizace a zpusob zivota' *Sociologie Mesta a Bydleni*, 1971, No. 7.

Winnick, L. B.: 'Housing: Has There Been a Downward Shift in Consumer Preferences?' *Quarterly Journal of Economics*, 1955, February, pp. 85–97 and 1956, May, pp. 314–23.

Wirth, Louis: *The Ghetto*, Chicago, The University of Chicago Press, 1928.

Wood, E. E.: 'A Century of the Housing Problem', *Law and Contemporary Problems*, 1934, March, pp. 137–323.

Young, M., and Willmott, P.: *Family and Kinship in East London*, New York, The Free Press, 1957.

Ziolkowski, Janusz: 'Towards a Sociology of Regional Development and Planning', *New Atlantis*, 1971, No. 2, pp. 30–58.

Zivkovic, Miroslav: 'Jedan primer segregacije u rázvohu nasik gradova', *Sociologija*, 1968, pp. 37–58.

Index